# Are You Persuaded?

# Are You Persuaded?

## In and Out of Being a Bishop

PORTER TAYLOR

*Foreword by Katharine Jefferts Schori*

RESOURCE *Publications* · Eugene, Oregon

ARE YOU PERSUADED?
In and Out of Being a Bishop

Resource Publications
An Imprint of Wipf and Stock Publishers
199 W. 8th Ave., Suite 3
Eugene, OR 97401

www.wipfandstock.com

PAPERBACK ISBN: 978-1-6667-5529-9
HARDCOVER ISBN: 978-1-6667-5530-5
EBOOK ISBN: 978-1-6667-5531-2

VERSION NUMBER 111722

To Jo
I have been persuaded that you are the love of my life since we met
fifty-three years ago.

Q: How is such a belief possible in this day and age?

A: What else is there?

Q: What do you mean, what else is there? There is humanism, atheism, agnosticism, Marxism, behaviorism, materialism, Muhammadanism, Sufism, astrology, occultism, theosophy.

A: That's what I mean.

—WALKER PERCY, "QUESTIONS THEY NEVER ASKED ME," *CONVERSATIONS WITH WALKER PERCY*

# Contents

# Foreword

PERSUASION IS A SPLIT personality thing for most human beings. Some of us are gullible, swallowing wholesale whatever is on offer. Some are unwilling to listen, heels dug in, never even examining the persuader's aim. Most are somewhere in between, wondering, unsure, wary, uninterested in sorting the depths. Yet the word itself comes from roots that mean something like *toward sweetness*. Being persuaded moves toward a sweet spot, recognizing congruent possibilities. Persuasion is the stuff of acceptance; it can't be imposed.

The sweetness of that internal congruency bespeaks finding and living a vocation, answering a deep call. Augustine of Hippo reportedly put it thus: "My heart is restless until it rests in thee, O Lord." Yet Augustine's *rest* is never a complete reality for any living human being until we return to the sod. At best, we have glimpses and seasons, living truth and conviction (mostly) that we're going in the right direction. Ecclesiastes calls it *vanity*, but the less usual translation of *mist* or *cloud* is more accurate. Our knowing is always partial, and so is the sweet spot, for it's never eternally fixed.

The journey recounted here is faithful, self-disclosing, and vulnerable. It is the fruit of decades of self-examination as well as doing what needs to be done—deep introspection and diligence even in drudgery. Porter's witness to the reader exposes the partial nature of all faithful leadership as well as moments of joy and revelation. The partial reality is especially true for spiritual leaders, who are set a bar of excellence, faithfulness, kindness, and availability that is impossible for any human being. Queen Elizabeth lived such a life, with the help of courts of aides and advisors. Bishops have fewer assistants, less funding, and serve shorter chapters, yet they have similar responsibilities—spiritual and moral leadership, leading and serving justice, and inspiring those in their orbit to greater expressions of humanity. Those are all about persuasive labor, and in more formal religious leadership, that work means loving people, systems, and communities into new places, new sweet spots, where love grows and expands, and makes more of itself.

The God of the Bible is a persuader, luring mortals into deeper relationship and recognition of their creator's reflection among their neighbors and fellow creatures. Jesus of Nazareth fished for people who were willing to imagine and realize communities of greater justice, which is what love looks like in public. God loves us into new realities, yet the result is never fully realized. As soon as a society begins to recognize the full humanity of one sort of person, we begin to see and ask about the many others still excluded from that sweet spot. The only truly faithful response is to keep on keeping on, channeling the persuading voice within, calling us to keep loving the world into greater sweetness for all. We will die before we get there, yet our witness can inspire and lure others to that persuading journey. This persuasive work entails suffering, *to carry or bear*, including the new lives that will follow us, for suffering is part of every life-giving journey. It can be the challenging bitterness that returns us to the search for sweetness.

Give thanks for Bishop Taylor's courageous and faithful example, and find yourself gently persuaded toward a new and lively sweetness in your own life journey.

— Katharine Jefferts Schori,
Presiding Bishop of The Episcopal Church (2005–2016)

# Preface

GROWING UP, MY FAMILY lived a few blocks from the bishop of Western North Carolina. I seldom saw him but imagined that somehow he had a clear channel to God. I can't say that I knew much more about the episcopacy until I was elected as the Bishop of Western North Carolina at the age of fifty-four. Maybe Kierkegaard was right when he wrote, "*Life* can only be *understood backwards*; but *it* must be *lived forwards*."[1] Having been retired from the episcopacy since 2016, I am beginning to understand what that vocation meant to me, and what I learned from it as well as sacrificed for it.

It was a great privilege to pastor to the faithful Episcopalians in Western North Carolina and to ordain men and women as deacons and priests. Moreover, I was honored to participate in the councils of the church as we elected Presiding Bishops and discerned the church's new efforts and objectives. I participated in some key moments of the church, especially as it pertains to the episcopacy: the confirmation of Gene Robinson to be the first gay person to be a bishop, and the election of Katharine Jefferts Schori as the first woman to be the head of the church followed by the election of Michael Curry as the first African American to hold that office. However, amid those amazing events, the everyday requirements of the office were not only exhausting but were often the catalyst for me losing my way.

This memoir offers a picture of what it can cost to grow in one's faith. Being a bishop affected my relationship with my wife, my children, my larger family, and my friends. On the other hand, it was an enormous vehicle for growth. I repeatedly had to remind myself that even though you have titles and vestments, you are always a sinner in need of God's redemption and a pilgrim seeking to walk in The Way.

There's a reason the early church was called "The Way." Our life with Christ is never stationary. I had to discern when to move to be ordained, to

---

1. Kierkegaard, "Soren Kierkegaards Skrifter," 306.

be a rector of a parish, to be a bishop, and to let go, and in some sense return to where I started. I have learned that the world is indeed round.

I have no regrets about this journey. I have been blessed in each phase. As Kierkegaard pointed out, having lived it forward, this book is a vehicle for understanding it backward.

# Acknowledgments

NO ONE GETS TO heaven by themselves. I am grateful to the many students I have had the privilege of teaching, especially the class on "Writing Your Memoir" at Wake Forest Divinity School. As always, I learned more than the students.

Likewise, I was privileged and blessed to have been part of the writing classes in the Great Smokies Writing Program in Asheville, North Carolina. My two teachers, Tommy Hayes and Elizabeth Lutyens not only helped my writing skills but were examples of creative and charitable teaching.

Thanks to the Collegeville Institute for their "Apart, and Yet a Part" internship and for Michael McGregor's insight.

I am grateful to all the people that affirmed this endeavor: Francie Thayer, my spiritual director; Judith Whelchel, my priest; and my men's group including Ron Rios, Bruce Grob, Jim Pritchett, and Dennis Fotinos.

This book would never have come about without my wonderful wife, Jo Taylor. She was patient and encouraging during the many years it took to finish this project. I am grateful for the support and love from my two children, Arthur and Marie.

Yet with all this help, it's all grace. My deepest acknowledgment is to the living God. St. Julian of Norwich reminded me on those days and years when I thought this would never happen that because God is God indeed, "But all will be well, and every kind of thing will be well."[1]

And so it is, and so it will be.

---

1. Colledge and Walsh, *Julian of Norwich Showings*, 149.

# Introduction

MY JOURNEY IN FAITH has not been in a straight line. Indeed, I had to move outside Christianity to come back and embrace not only Christianity but the church. To return to the church, I had to leave the church. Thus, my wife and I went to India. In Poona I visited the childhood home of Meher Baba and then St. Francis' small chapel, the Portiuncula, just below Assisi. Both places gave me a deep experience of the divine presence and caused radical reorientation. They enlarged my faith and propelled me to reinvestigate the church.

I knew I wanted to be a priest when I was in elementary school, but as an adolescent, I wasn't convinced that the church was wide enough or deep enough. However, in midlife, I realized that there is a point in which one's time is short, and, therefore, if one is going to pursue one's dream, the moment is the present. Thus, I went through the process of discernment to be an Episcopal priest and was sent to The School of Theology, known as Sewanee, in Tennessee.

There I discovered what it meant to be on the other side of the altar as well as how wide the church is. The Seminary had students who were liberal and conservative, low church and high church, spiritually oriented and politically oriented, plus introverted and extroverted. My time there helped me realize that there's some truth that The Episcopal Church is indeed the church of all sorts as well as reaffirming my call to the priesthood.

After seminary I was fortunate to serve in a friendly parish outside Nashville, Tennessee. My wife loved her job, my kids liked their schools, and we had a wonderful house. The people of St. Paul's, Franklin were creative, dedicated, and fun. However, my restlessness returned, and I felt called to move to a new city to serve as the rector of St. Gregory the Great Episcopal Church in Athens, Georgia.

In some ways I felt this period was the best fit for my gifts and the church's need. I kept rediscovering the truth that we live our lives forward and understand them backward. My return to the church did not come from an intellectual understanding of the gospels but rather experiences that convinced me that God was not an intellectual concept nor a winsome belief that no truly intelligent person could believe, but was a holy presence alive wherever we are. Indeed, most of the changes in my life have come from the heart center and not the head center. We moved to Athens, Georgia so I could be the rector of a medium-size church not because it made sense to leave Nashville, but because something about the people and their faith beckoned me.

While at St. Gregory the Great, I was elected to be a deputy at The Episcopal Church's General Convention in Minneapolis in 2004. I loved meeting people I had only read about, yet I became somewhat disillusioned by the governing process. Convention is an ecclesial House of Representatives and Senate. The bishops are the Senate, and the elected lay people and clergy are the House of Representatives. Despite a full agenda, the primary focus was whether to affirm The Rev. Gene Robinson as the bishop of New Hampshire. The process was messy because he is an openly gay man, and yet, as W.B. Yeats wrote, "A terrible beauty was born."[1]

I was comfortable at St. Gregory's and felt we were doing good work. I liked the congregation, and they liked me. In spite of that, I agreed to be on the ballot to be the bishop of Western North Carolina. This was partly because the headquarters are in Asheville, North Carolina where I grew up. I wasn't interested in going to another parish; I was interested in doing something different. Part of my story is a restlessness. I was surprised to be elected, and it was only afterward that I discovered what that meant for me and my wife, Jo, and our two children.

When I was ordained a bishop, the question that caused me to pause, even with the congregation sitting behind me and the ordaining bishop standing in front of me, was, "Are you persuaded that God has called you to the office of bishop?" After a lengthy process of being evaluated and questioned and finally elected by representatives of the parishes in the Episcopal Diocese of Western North Carolina, I realized that even as I was persuaded, I really didn't know what this meant, or indeed how the church institution worked, or if I had the essential qualities.

In ordination the church points to an "ontological change." However, the change I experienced was the wide range of expectations suddenly placed on me. I wasn't any wiser as a bishop than I was as a priest or layperson, but I instantly became the mayor, the police, the counselor, the financial guru, and the garbage man. Of course, I was still just me.

---

1. Yeats, "Easter 1916," 177.

Being a bishop meant being included in events in the church which I had never considered. I traveled extensively and, therefore, became an important person to American Airlines. I was so surprised when I retired that they no longer seemed to care about me at all. I traveled to India, England, Scotland, Taiwan, Puerto Rico, Ecuador, as well as the east and west coasts of the United States. I was sincerely honored to be in this position even as I often wondered how and why I got there.

Perhaps the highlight of my episcopacy was to vote for Michael Curry and Katharine Jefferts Schori as consecutive Presiding Bishops. Both broke barriers, a man of color and a woman, and both brought amazing gifts to the church. It was an enormous privilege to be part of these two events, especially as I was on the committee that counted the votes in Bishop Katharine's election.

While the workload was massive, the people of The Diocese of Western North Carolina were always kind and helpful. The foundation of most of my encounters with the laity and the clergy was a desire to live into what God was calling us to do and to be. Indeed, one of my regrets was being too busy to connect with the laity and clergy at a deeper level.

However, there was the other side to this office. I found myself doing too many things in too many different places. In addition, while I have certain gifts, it seldom seemed as if I was called to use them. I kept having to rely on my non-dominant hand. In the short term, this pushed me to grow, but in the long term it was exhausting. Perhaps if I had said "no" more often, I would have found a doable pace, but that has never been my strong suit.

After twelve years, I decided I could no longer be the active bishop of The Episcopal Church in Western North Carolina. It wasn't the people; they were wonderful. I was just tired and had little enthusiasm for what needed to be done. Yes, I was honored to have served in this office, but I could feel that the institution was taking away my ability to be the person I was born to be. I was less creative and too often weary.

This book points to my next step. After retiring, I taught at Wake Forest Divinity School for three years and rediscovered my enthusiasm for engaging with people about ideas concerning our souls and our connection to the divine source. Do I miss being the diocesan bishop? Not often. Admittedly, it's been a challenge to sit in the pews and be content with the worship as it is and not as I think it could or should be. In truth, I had to recall my true calling from my baptism: "To seek and serve Christ in all persons, loving your neighbor as yourself."[2] I had to deal with not representing an institution which is both freeing and isolating. After teaching at Wake

---

2. *The Book of Common Prayer*, 305.

Forest, I did return to being active as an assistant bishop for the Episcopal Diocese of Virginia, but it's hard to compare that with my previous calling. I was an assistant and not the final authority. In addition, this was all during COVID-19.

I don't know what the future holds in terms of me and the church. I go to a wonderful parish every Sunday and occasionally preach. I am a Spiritual Director and counsel various folks, and I have been teaching a class back at Wake Forest Divinity School. However, I find that it's better for my soul if I am no longer in charge. I am more in the moment because I am not trying to make anything work out, except my dog's barking, which seems to be a long-range endeavor.

Am I still persuaded? Well, not to be active as bishop, but I am always persuaded that when God calls us and asks us, "Can you serve in this way?" the answer, even with a long pause, is "Yes." Then we see what happens and sometimes understand what God has in mind. As the Psalmist says, "Taste and see the goodness of the Lord." Even when I have been lost and wondered why I was chosen to fill a certain office, I try to remember that I am not in charge. On my best days I am an instrument for God and Christ in the Holy Spirit, but even on my worst days, I still say "Yes" to what the Spirit sometimes faintly whispers in my soul. Because I am now in my seventh decade of life, I realize I don't have time to wrestle with being persuaded. Instead, when the Holy Spirit whispers in our hearts, those who seek to be faithful even knowing our limitations and the inconvenience, must say, "Yes." In the end, to be faithful is to be persuaded because God's persuasion enables us to be faithful and to grow.

# 1

# Tourist or Pilgrim

He who seeks to know the ground on which we stand and its as yet inviolate
treasure is doomed to go abroad through the world.

—ELIZABETH SEWELL, *SIGNS AND CITIES*

I WALKED INTO THE room and ran into the wall. Not a figurative one but
a plaster pink one. The pink room was so small I could almost touch both
walls. What was this room for—laundry?

One lamp hung down from the ceiling. There was no furniture just
bare pink walls and a concrete floor painted white. I walked in and had to
turn to my left because there was nowhere else to go.

At the end of the room, maybe fifteen feet away, I saw a stone about
the size of a brain cemented into the floor. It stuck up maybe four inches.
I couldn't tell what kind of rock it was because like so much of the ground
in India, it was grayish brown. I took one step toward it, then another, then
one more.

No one else was in the room. For a moment, I wondered, "Why am I
here? What could go on? What could happen in a place so small?"

Above the stone, there was a kind of altar with pink and white flowers
roped into a garland and candles—not our Christian votive candles but tall
ones like those for the Lady of Guadalupe. A small round ceramic dome
held two sticks with plumes of incense twirling toward the ceiling. The
smoke burned my eyes and caught in my throat.

What was I doing in Pune, India, in a pink closet, staring at a rock?

That question made me turn away. This was foolish. My parents' objection, "You are abandoning your roots," came back with a whoosh. That old refrain of "I can't do anything right," was the counter whisper that sucked me dry.

But here I was. I decided not to look at the smallness of the room or the garish candles or the stone or the pink or anything. I decided to close my eyes and breathe. To close out the voices in my head, I repeated "Peace, peace, peace" with every in and out of my breath. Over and over. "Peace, peace, peace."

A crooked road had led me to this place. The 1970s were my religious wandering period. I liked the idea of church in a nostalgic way, but I couldn't get there on Sundays. It was too much like my father's world. Too button down; too linear; too stiff. Yet, I struggled to find something else.

That something else began when I was a sophomore in college. I was sitting in the living room of the Beta House at the University of North Carolina, Chapel Hill, reading my Shakespeare, when Jack Johnson, a fraternity brother from Winston-Salem, came up to me and out of the blue said, "I don't need this book anymore. Why don't you take it?"

I stared at him because I didn't really know him. I knew he was an English major, but he was a senior and quiet and kept to himself—like me. He stood in front of me with a "Question Authority" button on his black T-shirt, holding a brown paperback in his hand.

"Sure. Thanks." The book cover showed an older man with a wide grin making an okay sign with his fingers. I wondered if Jack thought I was the only one weird enough to want to read this. The book was *The Everything and the Nothing* by Meher Baba. It turned out to be similar to Hinduism—reincarnation, the world is illusion, there is an alternate reality where we are one.

I was in this in-between place. I was an English major, but I was taking more religion classes than literature. Sometimes I would go to the empty Episcopal Church to sit and think late at night and stare at the altar lit by one lone light and long to feel something, but I couldn't bear to sit through Sunday morning services. I was a seeker without a map.

After I read the book, I asked Jack about it. "I don't know" he said. "I found it at the Intimate Bookshop. But I heard that there is actually a center for Meher Baba in Myrtle Beach." As I read, I found that Meher Baba died in 1969 and kept silent for the last forty-four years of his life.

"Let me get this right. Myrtle Beach—Pavilion, Gay Dolphin, Arcade, and a spiritual center?"

I didn't think about this too much for a while, but one weekend in 1970 when my family was at Pawleys Island, I drove north on Highway 17 through the ticky-tacky long section of amusement rides, sunglasses stores, restaurants with waiting lines of elderly couples and parents with squirming children, and miniature golf courses on every corner to a stretch of Highway 17 that was an empty two-lane road. I turned onto a side street and came to a brick ranch house where Kitty Davy, one of the leaders of the Meher Spiritual Center, lived.

Kitty was an eighty-year-old English woman. She asked me in for tea. It was June and hot. I walked into her office wondering what I could say to someone that old and that unique. After all, this woman left London to live in nowhere India for decades. The top of Kitty's head came to my chin. To see me, she crooked her head to the left and looked up. Her smile covered her face. She reached her hands up to me and patted my cheeks as if I were a schoolboy. I couldn't believe how large her hands were for such a small woman.

"Sit down, sit down," she said. I sat down in a blue vinyl chair facing her across her desk. I was looking for Lipton or maybe Twinings, but we were served chai—strong, sweet, thick—and Pepperidge Farm cookies. I drank and ate and looked at her hairline because I was too timid to look her in the eyes. Kitty talked a bit about how she met this master in the 1930s and how she had lived in India. Finally, she wore down and appeared to look all the way through me. "What brings you here?"

What had brought me here? I couldn't say. I blurted, "Meher Baba. How do you know he's the one?"

"Well," she said in her lilting voice. "Well. Because when I was with Baba, I knew what it was to be alive."

I wanted that. More than anything I wanted to know what it was to be alive and to be connected to the source. I wrote in my journal, "Holy One, come to me without a name. Touch me with what is real and true." I didn't know the Holy One's name, but my need was so great, I didn't care about the name. I knew that too much of the time I felt frozen inside. I would go anywhere to get thawed out.

I read Meher Baba's books and occasionally went to the Center in Myrtle Beach during the '70s. For me, most of this decade was a kind of spiritual walkabout. I affirmed all kinds of universal principles, but the church felt too small for the universal God.

In the late '70s I was back on the outskirts of the church—not going on Sunday but sometimes going to a Friday morning Eucharist after I volunteered at a homeless shelter all night. I knew I wanted to be fed, but I wasn't sure about the baggage. A stripped-down service—no sermon, no coffee hour, no questions—just the bread and the prayers were all I could handle. I could not find the deep water but was weary of swimming in the shallow end.

In 1981 I was still primarily untethered, ungrounded, and unanimated. I was in a PhD program without really knowing why. I had quit my high school teaching job because I was going through the motions, not because I was called to something else. I was just in between. Not clear about career, unresolved with family, drifting in spirit. I wanted an experience. I yearned to believe in something, anything, but could not commit with all my heart. Church felt like a Rotary Club meeting, but everything else felt made up. I could not find solid ground.

I realized that graduate school gave me a month off around Christmas. I said to my wife, Jo, "How about going to India?" and called a travel agent. I wanted to see about Meher Baba for myself. As I was talking to the woman on the phone, she said, "There's a return flight that goes from Bombay to Rome to New York." I knew Jo had to get home because she had a real job, but there's freedom to being a perpetual student. "Can you get off the plane in Rome?" I asked. We decided to go together to India, but I would get off on the way back.

And here we were. Pune, India. The first night in the hotel I couldn't sleep. First the noises never stopped. Muslim calls to prayer, strange sharp bird calls, low rumbling diesel trucks, and the piercing chirps of horns on the motorcycle bumblebees that carried two people in a carriage. The whole room was white tile. It was like being in a big bathroom. The only light was a single bulb. The toilet was a hole in the floor. It took a long consultation for me to figure out how this worked. That night I wrote, "I am scared I will slide off the world. This is the land where anything is possible."

When we went down for breakfast, our waiter, a short man whose dark Indian skin contrasted with his bright, starched, white uniform, brought us chai and then disappeared. Moments later we heard an Indian version of the theme song from *Goldfinger* sounding from the ceiling. It was his gesture to make us feel at home. He returned expectant, but I couldn't eat. I was too wired and too everything.

That morning we went sightseeing in Pune from the safe distance of our taxi, but the distance didn't feel safe enough. I saw women cooking over fires next to tin shacks and men squatting in the field for their morning constitutional. Children with haunting eyes that you don't want to remember. The smells—some pungent mixture of smoke, dung, and diesel that catches in your throat and mixes into your clothes. Then this jangle of sounds— constant horns from trucks, cars, and bicycles; atonal music blaring from loudspeakers; and the low rumble of strange dialects. Our little cab was a bubble of order amid this foreign land.

Kitty Davy had told me that Meher Baba grew up in Pune, and you could visit his house—called Pumpkin House. When I asked the cab driver if he could get us there, he wobbled his head, but I couldn't tell if that was "Yes" or "No." I tried to pretend I trusted him. On the cab's dashboard was a statue of Krishna with incense in the ashtray. Riding through the streets I looked at the women hanging their bright saris on wash lines, the cows with their dull stare, and the children—always children with hands outstretched.

When we turned onto a side street for the house, there was no marker, only the number. I wasn't sure we were in the right place, and there was no one around. I wondered if it was wise to leave the cab, but we couldn't stay in limbo forever. We paid an inexplicable amount of rupees—which oddly enough looks like Monopoly money. We walked through a cobblestone patio and knocked on the front door. A short, plump woman in a green sari greeted us. Her hair was parted in the center with a red splash on her forehead. "Pumpkin house?" I asked. "Yes, yes," she said, as she wobbled her head from side to side and ushered us in.

The house reminded me of a small version of our American ranch houses in the 1950s. There were photos of the master's family everywhere. Walking around was kind of interesting, but only kind of. As always, I was done before Jo. I am either a quick study or lack sufficient curiosity because I always finish sightseeing quickly. I turned to go back to the courtyard and saw a doorway to a small room to my right.

I later learned that when Baba had his revelation at an early age, he would go into this room and bang his head on the stone now fixed into the floor. Apparently, his spiritual states were so intense, he had to jolt himself back into his body and this world.

When I walked into the room, I hit the pink wall and turned to my left. Alone in the room I took three steps forward, stopped, closed my eyes, and said over and over: "Peace."

I began to breathe. I felt my muscles relax and realized I had been clenched down in a defensive stance since the airplane landed. I uncrossed my arms and let them dangle at my side. "Peace, peace, peace."

I opened my eyes and looked at the gray-brown rock in the floor. "Peace." No words. No explanations. No judgment. No analysis. "Peace."

For a few moments I just basked in a relaxation I had not known since boarding the airplane. I was able to circle my head and hear the creaks and cracks of my neck. I circled my shoulders frontward and then backward. "Peace." Again, "peace."

Slowly I felt an energy come into my body. It was as if I was being lifted from the floor. I felt a quickening of what it is to be alive. I still looked at the rock, but the color of the room intensified, and I became warmer. So, I closed my eyes and began to take deeper, slower breaths. "Peace."

The more I breathed, the more intense the energy became. Suddenly, I felt an electric current run through me. It was not a gentle reassurance. I was not being strangely warmed. It felt like being hit in the solar plexus. My breath got shorter and shorter. I opened my eyes and the room looked translucent. It seemed to be pulsing with my heartbeat.

In an inexplicable way, I felt a draw toward the rock like a magnetic pull, but I also felt an instinctive pull not to go there. It was a primal fear. I knew that I could handle no more of this.

I stood still to see if the current would subside, but it did not. So, I pushed my feet backward and I held my arms in front of me as if to ward something off. I backed out of the room. When I crossed the threshold, I immediately felt released.

I was breathing deep breaths with my mouth wide open. My back to the pink room, I let my eyes roam in the living room, but I could not focus. Jo came up to me and said, "Are you ready?" Then she looked at me. "You okay?"

"Let's get out of here."

The rest of my Indian trip was prosaic. It was informative and entertaining but not electric. No one helped me make sense of the pink room. It was an experience without explanation. Did it validate Meher Baba? Did it mean I was crazy? Was it leading me deeper into India or back home to the comfort of Christianity, and if I chose to return to Christianity, would I ever have such an experience again?

I had this experience, but I didn't know what it meant. It pushed me off center and made me know that the God hunger is not an intellectual, much less aesthetic, search for a religion that made sense. The pink room made no sense, but it was real. I knew Meher Baba was deeper than I could imagine, but I didn't know what that meant.

\* \* \*

Why is it that I am writing about this trip? Yes, it was a turning point. I went from India to Assisi in Italy, and something also happened there. But at my age I thought I was done with turning. After that trip, I rejoined the church and ten years later became an Episcopal priest. Eleven years after that I was ordained a bishop. For years I represented the institution. In many ways, where I lived, I was the face of the church. People thought my first name was "Bishop" not "Porter." The pink room and the pink city of Assisi seemed as if they were about another person in another time.

Many years later, I went to a four-day meeting in Memphis with twenty other bishops. The meeting was at the Hilton near the airport. For six hours, I sat in The Admiral Conference room, cream-colored with no windows, hearing about health insurance. A sharp middle-aged guy with gray-spiked hair and goatee, from Hartford, Connecticut, kept going over the tables to explain why our diocese had to pay higher premiums because we had too many old white men as priests.

"It's all about the actuarial tables," he said. "We know you will have more claims than the clergy living in Massachusetts because they are younger."

"That's a hard sell for me to say to the clergy—you live in the wrong place, so your insurance is high," I said.

His reply was, "Well, in that case your problem is less financial than political."

*What am I doing here?*

On Sunday of that week, I put on my purple shirt and cape and miter and ring and pectoral cross and held my crozier just in case I needed to yank back any heretics and keep the flock in line as I entered one of the historically Black Episcopal Churches in Rutherfordton, North Carolina. The ladies who greeted me at the door were all grandmothers and dressed to impress. "Bishop, we are so glad to see you. Can I get you some water? Do you know where your chair is? Would you like to meet the Senior Warden? We made a cake just for your visitation." I felt like the pope.

But at the end of the service, as I was walking to my car, one elderly lady in a bright peacock blue dress with a matching hat walked toward me holding the hand of a small boy about five years old. He wore khaki pants, a blue blazer, and a clip-on bow tie. I could tell he was stretching his grandmother's arm to get behind her. "Bishop, I am Helen Smith, and this is my grandson, Thomas. He's got no father, and his momma is addicted to cocaine, and we don't know where she is. Will you give him your blessing?"

I knelt before Thomas and laid my hands on his head. "May the Lord bless you and keep you. May the Lord be gracious to you. And Thomas, may the Lord give you peace now and always."

I looked up. "Thank you, Helen. It's an honor to meet your grandson."

I thought of the pink room and wondered what happened to me, but when I thought of the saint from Assisi, and of my knee touching the ground to bless and be blessed, I held on to hope. There's a legend about Francis of Assisi, that before his death, he said to his friars: "Up to now we have done

nothing, let's begin again." I was more than aware of how little I had done. I
prayed to begin again.

* * *

Jo and I flew to Rome side by side. We left Mumbai at three in the morning,
so we didn't talk much. She slept with her head on my shoulder, while I
read *Middlemarch* with a flashlight. What would Dorothea do with the pink
room? We landed in Rome sometime after dawn. I walked Jo to her gate for
the New York leg and said goodbye.

When I came out of the Rome airport, I was hit by the cold. It was
midmorning and January gray. I got into a cab but didn't know what to tell
the driver because I had no destination.

"Train station," I said. On route I looked in my guidebook for hotels,
circling the cheapest with my red grading pen. Of course, I couldn't figure
out the phones. I couldn't tell if it was ringing or busy. I had to keep buying
Cokes from the newsstand to get change. I tried three. "No rooms. Sorry.
No rooms."

It was getting colder, and the wind was picking up. In desperation, I
went to the train station and stood in the ticket line. I was behind six people,
all shorter than me and all with hats or shawls. I looked above the line of
heads at the board over the counter and saw "Assisi."

"Of course. That's why I am here," I thought.

I had read G.K. Chesterton's book on the life of St. Francis of Assisi
before I left. My interest in him was more about how he dealt with his family's rejection than his love of animals. The train left at 4:40 p.m. and arrived
at 7:30 p.m.

I got lunch and coffee and paid 500 lire to use the toilet. When I came
back to the station about four o'clock, I could not be reassured that I was on
the right track. I kept asking strangers, "Assisi?" "Si, Assisi," and they would
point to the track number. They had dealt with people like me before.

The train car held five Italians and me. A mother and her two children
sat across from me with their basket of bread, cheese, and olives. I tried not
to lick my lips or play Oliver Twist. After a little while the mother opened
the window, which baffled me. It was January and now dark outside. Then I
realized, it wasn't the heat but the smell from this Indian traveler. I had been
awake for thirty-six hours and had not bathed in more than that.

The train arrived at a dark Assisi station. Three or four others got off.
The station was in the valley. I looked up to the lights of promise. My guidebook told of a convent, and I had called from Rome. I got out of the cab,

went up the walk, and rang the bell. In a few moments, a short nun wearing a large black veil with wings, looking as if she belonged in *The Sound of Music*, let me in. She showed me to my small room—one bed, one chair, one table. Quiet but cold. I put on a sweatshirt over my pajamas and slept like the dead.

When I woke, the light poured through the window. I looked outside and saw a pink city. The marble of Assisi glowed with the morning light. The city sat on a hill facing the rising sun. It was luminescent. Unlike the clangor of India, here was a stillness and a calmness and a welcoming soft light. Instead of the hot pulsating pinkness of the Indian room was the pink of morning sunrise glow. Breakfast was served in a basement dining room. No one else was there. I sat at a long wooden table, no linen, no flowers. A nun came in with a plate of eggs and a cup of coffee and placed them before me.

"Tourist or pilgrim?" she asked. Surprisingly, she had a British accent.

"Not sure."

"Well," she said, "I hope you find whatever it is you are looking for."

"Thank you, Sister, but right now, all I am looking for is this coffee."

I spent three days seeing the sights. I often found myself alone in places that would be jammed in the summer. I was an undisciplined seeker. In the morning I had no clear idea of the day. I just started. I walked from one sight to the next and sat and stared. "Peace," I said, not to invoke it, but to name what I felt. "Peace, peace."

Each day I went to a restaurant on one corner of the square and sat at the table by the window so I could see where Francis left his family for his new life. The room was filled with square tables and had an old-world look— starched white napkins, two forks, two glasses, the works. The waiter wore a white shirt, black vest, black pants. He would come and ask something in Italian. I simply said, "Si" and he brought food. I didn't know the name of anything; I just ate it. I was learning by ingestion and not abstraction. It was so cold, I learned to eat slowly to stay inside as long as possible. I never knew when the meal was over until the waiter brought the bill. Sometimes it was soup, main course, desert; sometimes not. Whatever came, I ate.

I wandered in a kind of daze. I was not in India. I was not home. I was here. Most days I went to the Basilica of San Francesco to see the life of Saint Francis laid out on the walls in frescoes of deep blues and rosy reds. The Giotto frescoes are more than beautiful. You can't simply admire them. There's not a way to observe them. They draw you in. They are a kind of bridge to the way this little man of Assisi walked. I stared at the fresco showing Pope Innocent III asleep while Francis holds up St. Peter's Cathedral with his shoulder. The story is that Francis walked to Rome and asked the Pope to allow an order of poor men to be formed. The Pope refused, and then dreamed that the magnificent cathedral was toppling over only to be held up by the poor man from Assisi. He called Francis back and the Franciscans were created.

Every day in the late afternoon I went to the Basilica of St. Clare to hear the nuns sing. They processed in—maybe twenty of them—and circled the casket where dead St. Clare lay—her black skull outlined by the white lining of her black veil. The church was dark and there was a rood screen or grill between the congregation and the nuns. With their habits, only their faces were visible but when they sang, the sound washed everything else away. Clear, light, high tones. All Latin, which could be saying anything and everything. The only way to understand it was note by note.

I spent my days in a consoling routine. I walked and sat and ate at my restaurant and then walked and sat and ate. I saw all the sights, but I was hardly a tourist. I didn't take pictures. I didn't read guidebooks. I simply wandered and wondered. I had no clarity except that here I could breathe, and here I could sleep, and here I could follow my feet, and wherever they led was more than okay. It was where I needed to be.

On the fourth day, one of the nuns, short and overweight, asked me if I'd been to the Porziuncola. I didn't know if it was a bar or another country. Her accent had a Germanic tone as she gave an exacting direction: "You must go there. It's a holy place." I started to ask her if it had a pink room, but instead I wrote down instructions. The guidebook told me the name meant "little piece." I got on the right bus, and it wound its way down the Umbrian hill to the valley. I found myself in front of an enormous white marbled church that looked the size of the National Cathedral. As I drew closer to the entrance, over the door I saw a large golden Madonna with her arms stretched wide in welcome. I walked through the entrance and found myself in a huge space that was magnificent but remarkably plain. The ceiling had magnificent frescoes, but the walls were largely white. The church was the length of a football field, its floor of a rose and white marble in a diamond pattern that went on forever. At the other end between the congregation and the altar was a small building. I could see that it was painted, but from the distance I couldn't make out any design.

A building within a building? As I drew near, I saw red Joseph and blue Mary over the doorway. "It's the church within the church," I whispered. The building is twenty feet by twelve. It still had the rock foundations that Francis used in the early thirteenth century. The small altar was black wood, some of the wood Francis used nine centuries before. There was a glorious splash of color above it, but the side walls were bare stone most of the way up. The floor was stone. Solid ground. No windows, no decoration. A place to stand, walls to lean on. There was a bright picture of the holy family on the altar, but I wasn't interested in that. I wasn't looking for decoration. I was looking for what would last.

When Francis understood that the only way to find himself was to leave home and look for a new father, he came here. He renounced his father by taking all his possessions and throwing them on the ground in the middle of town. When his father in anger renounced him as his son, Francis replied that he had no father but God the Father. He knew that Christ had told him from the cross at St. Clare's to build Christ's Church, but he didn't join anything, and he didn't get ordained. He walked away from home and city and came to the flat ground of the valley and laid these stones. Stone by stone into something that would last and be a place for a wayward pilgrim like me to put my feet and find my way.

Francis frequently came back here when he was tired or discouraged or maybe when he could find no other place for his happiness. The biographies say it was his favorite place in the world. Maybe it reminded him of his beginning or maybe it offered a perspective of his city and the house he had left. Maybe he could see his father more clearly from below. At the end of his short life on October 3, 1226, at the age of forty-four, this is where he came to die because he wanted to die at home—at his only true home. The legends say that he died in a small cell next to the chapel. Before he died, he asked his brother friars to take off his clothes so he could die touching the earth, dust to dust. His last words to his friars were, "I have done what was mine to do, may Christ now teach you what you are to do."[1]

I sat in a chair by the wall and leaned into the jagged stone. I was a long way from the pink room. I wasn't trying to get electrified. I was looking for a Church within the Church. I was looking for foundation. I was trying to find what I was to do—laying stone by stone like Francis. I was trying to find a way to trust this institution called the Church.

Martin Luther said the Church is the Queen of Heaven and the Whore of Babylon both at once. Three hundred years after Francis died, people still flocked to Assisi. In fact, historians estimate that in the late 1500s, more than 100,000 visited the Porziuncola each year. Pope Pius V commissioned a church to build on top of the small chapel to boost the Franciscan movement but also to glean more money from the indulgences gained from pilgrims. Heaven and Babylon. So, this giant sanctuary was built over the one place that Francis loved even though Francis forbid his friars to build monuments. Legends are that when he would return, the friars would have built some dormitory, and Francis would tear it apart stone by stone, board by board.

1. St. Bonaventure, *The Life of Saint Francis*, 150.

If I rejoined the Church, would I become one of those friars building something artificial on top of what is true, or could I find my own Porziuncola? Would I be better off with the formless energy of the pink room even if it got me electrocuted? No, sitting in this "little piece," I knew I was where I belonged. Not electric but solid and true. I did not know how to find this once I crossed back over the ocean, but I would try.

# 2

# The Call

So what is being offered to you is not merely a choice amongst new states
of consciousness . . . but above all else a larger and intenser life . . . a total
consecration to the interests of the Real.

—EVELYN UNDERHILL, *PRACTICAL MYSTICISM*

"WHY DO YOU WANT to be a priest?"

I sat at the end of a long table staring at the questioner, the chair of the
committee—a rotund man wearing a black clergy shirt, round clergy collar,
and what looked like an expensive dark gray suit. He finished his question
by putting an arm of his glasses in his mouth. From the way he cocked his
head, I thought he had an answer in mind, but I had no idea what it was.
Eleven other men and women sat around the conference table waiting for
my reply. I looked down and bit my lip. I rubbed my right index finger and
right thumb back and forth.

The silence hadn't reached an awkward place, but it was closing in.

There was a lot at stake for me. This was the interview by the Commission on Ministry—the committee that decides which men and women to
recommend to the bishop for seminary and to be ordained as an Episcopal
priest. I only knew one of these people—a middle-aged woman with whom
I had worked on a Christian Education Conference. She had winked at me
as we made introductions, but now I was on my own. The men around the

table looked like they worked for the FBI, and the women looked like they belonged to the Junior League. Buttoned down and in the lines.

We were at the Diocesan Office Center in Nashville, Tennessee, in a spacious room that had once been a dining room. The interview was to be an hour; we were ten minutes in.

The woman next to me reached out her hand and touched my arm. I noticed her bright red nails against my dark gray suit. My only suit.

"Do you need a minute?" she asked in a hushed voice.

"No, no, no," I said in a whoosh. "It's just that I know there's a more sophisticated answer than I am going to give. I should talk about presiding at the Eucharist, and servant ministry, and being a Christ bearer or wounded healer, but the real answer for me is this: 'I think my being a priest would make God happy and I know it would make me happy.'"

They kind of leaned forward, saying in body language, "AND?"

"I mean, I love the idea of it all. Sermons, church services, hospital visits, Sunday school, weddings, funerals, acolytes, youth groups—the whole deal. I've wanted to be a priest since I was a kid."

The committee relaxed. I wasn't off the reservation after all.

A woman dressed in a deep blue dress at the far end said, "You are thirty-eight. Tell us why it took you so long."

"Well, I took some detours and honestly, it's that Groucho Marx thing about not wanting to be part of a club that would have me as a member. I mean I have always loved Jesus but have not been clear about being able to represent the church as an institution."

They asked about my life story, my connection to the church, my hobbies, my job. It was fine. No trick questions. No one asked about Thomas Cranmer or William White. In 1988 no one asked about ordaining gays and lesbians.

"What makes you love the church?"

"What does your wife think about being a clergy spouse?"

"What are your favorite hymns?"

When my hour was up, I had no idea if I had given them the right answers, but as I was rising out of my seat, the woman with the red fingernails leaned toward me and whispered, "You did fine."

* * *

I first thought about being a priest when I was six. My mother was on the altar guild at Trinity Church in Asheville, North Carolina. Saturday was her day to arrange the flowers on the altar and lay out the vessels—the silver chalice and plate and linens—for the Sunday service. Because my father worked Saturday mornings, sometimes my sister, brother, and I got dragged to church.

In 1956 the sense of mystery in church sanctuaries hadn't evaporated. Trinity Church was cool and dark. Sometimes I would sit in a pew about halfway down the aisle next to one of the massive stone pillars. I would watch the women quietly working, their heads illuminated by the floodlights. The footsteps of the women around the altar echoed. I heard them whispering about their work. The altar was tan marble. A solid block. An anchor. As the women placed candles and white starched linens and draped the chalice in a stiff green cloth, the space went from stark to mysterious.

One day when they were finished, I crept up to the wooden rail in front of the altar and knelt down. Even at six I felt displaced in my family. The only child with a strange name: Granville in a sea of Richards and Sarahs. In this place I felt oddly safe and awed—less a sense of call and more a sense of belonging.

* * *

When I left home for college, I left the church. I wasn't making a statement. I wasn't declaring my independence from family expectations. I just stopped. Sunday mornings were times for sleeping and newspapers, and in college, recovering from Saturday night. It was like having amnesia. I forgot church. I couldn't speak its language and I couldn't remember why it had been part of my life.

I became a "Christmas/Easter" Episcopalian. I was in for the nostalgia and covering over the many divides between myself and my parents. And it was fine. It was like going to a museum or reading a book you once enjoyed but know the plot too well to savor it again.

The odd thing was, the God hunger didn't leave me.

Just before I graduated from college, I drove to my hometown, Asheville, to see the bishop of the Episcopal Diocese of Western North Carolina. The bishop was an immovable force—short, stocky, with a deep voice and sharp blue eyes. I sat across the desk from him in his office in Black Mountain. His purple shirt sleeves were rolled up.

"I'd like to be a priest," I said.

Because Bishop Henry had known me most of my life, he used my nickname, Bam, instead of my given name. In fact, everyone did because it's hard to call a four-year-old "Granville" or "Porter."

"Well, Bam, I've known you all your life. Know your family. Good people. Tell me where you've been going to church since you left home."

I felt the heat come into my face. *What an idiot I am*, I thought. "The truth is Bishop, I haven't been going to church."

He cocked his head and stared at me. "Well, son. You figure that out and get back to me, how's that?"

I didn't get back to him because there was nothing to report.

I swapped going to church for reading about mystics—all kinds: Christian, Hindu, Taoist, Buddhist. I became interested in Meher Baba, an Indian master who was believed to be another Christ. Eventually I went to Emory University to study Christian mysticism and mystical poetry. I read Martin Buber and St. John of the Cross. I wrote papers on Paul Tillich and George Herbert. But Sunday mornings my ritual was listening to National Public Radio, reading the *New York Times*, and eating Krispy Kreme doughnuts.

* * *

My second year of graduate school at Emory I signed up for a yearlong course on Dante. I walked into a conference room the first day of class and took my seat at a square table that filled the room and seated about sixteen. At the head was a short man with a full head of gray hair. As he lifted his hands from his lap to open his notebook, I saw that they shook. *Parkinson's* I thought.

"Dear class, we are going to take a journey through hell and purgatory to get to heaven. Be warned," he said, "you won't just read about a character named Dante who goes on a mythic journey. If you open up, you'll find out it really is our common journey."

He looked around the room. "So, it doesn't matter what your religion is, or your faith is, just know that if you open this book, you will be changed."

My eyes got wider, and my heart got softer. "Who talks like that?" I wondered.

I discovered that the professor was a deep Roman Catholic—the Thomas Merton kind. After one of our classes, he told me to read *The Sermons on the Song of Songs* by Saint Bernard of Clairvaux, and I said, "What's the Song of Songs?"

"Bam," he said, "clearly no one told you the Bible is part family history, part love story, and most of all poetry."

Each class opened with a student giving a report on a canto of whatever book of *The Divine Comedy* we were reading. Emory also has a Methodist seminary on its campus; most graduate courses are cross listed. There was one seminarian in the Dante class. He was from South Georgia. He had big hands and a large round face.

He started his report by saying, "I don't know why Dante only talks about sin all the time. After all, the Good News is about grace. It's not about damnation but salvation."

I stared at my notebook. It got worse. The student walked us through the plot of the canto as if we couldn't decipher what the author was describing. When he finished, I looked around the room. Most of us had expressions of embarrassment. "What do you say to that?" I wondered. The student next to me was overly competitive. He should have been in law school because he challenged every student's assertion. I could hear him clearing his throat, ready to launch.

But our professor looked at the student and broke in with his soft voice, "Tell us about your journey. What took you to seminary and what are your plans after."

We stared at Dr. Evans as if he were speaking Italian. This was graduate school? But then I realized he had a larger agenda than reading the text. I saw that he was now teaching us what he had learned from Dante. And I felt smaller from my instincts and inclinations, but with a different horizon. I wondered if there was more to being a faithful Christian than I thought. I didn't know you could be intellectually respectable and go to church, and I hadn't seen many examples of this degree of kindness in academia.

\* \* \*

One day, a conversation, a throwaway line, made my life turn.

I was sitting on the bench in front of the Institute of Liberal Arts classroom in 1983, running my finger down the book page. I had ten minutes to read the assignment, but I discovered that although Levi Strauss was a famous anthropologist, he was incapable of writing a simple sentence.

"Hey, Bam. It looks like that church you gave up on may have some life in it after all."

"Oh hey, you mean the Frozen Chosen are thawing out?"

She and I were both working on our doctorates in Literature and Theology at Emory. She was a Catholic nun but the Sally Fields kind, not the kind who hammered kids' hands with rulers. No, she never tried to convert me, but she tried to find ways to coax me back into the big tent of the church.

"So, let's hear the good news about Episcopalians," I said.

She sat beside me. I wasn't sure if her blue skirt with matching jacket was her official nun's outfit. "They are starting a homeless shelter up at St.

Bart's—the Episcopal Church up the street. It will be the only family shelter in this part of the city."

She nudged my arm with hers. "Why don't you check it out?"

Two weeks later I was a volunteer on Thursday nights at St. Bart's. It wasn't a hard sell. Jo and I didn't have kids. She was glad to have me out one night a week so she could spend time in her art studio. I went because I felt too locked into my head. I liked the Emory program, but I was getting lopsided with so much abstraction.

The parish hall of St. Bartholomew's Episcopal Church was octagonal. Obviously from the '60s. Walking in right on time at five-thirty, I was greeted by the only person I knew from the church—a short middle-aged woman. She had an Emory connection and reminded me of one of the godmothers in the Cinderella cartoon: round, happy, fun. "Hey, Bam," she exclaimed. "Welcome to the best ministry in Atlanta."

St. Bart's had room for eight families—one per classroom. There were two showers plus a washer and dryer. Families could stay for up to two weeks, so the turnover was low.

My job was to sign people in at the six o'clock arrival time, which didn't sound hard. All eight families were returning.

I sat at a small wooden desk and felt like a librarian. The first family looked like Eskimos bundled in many layers. Early November in Atlanta has unpredictable weather. The night was cold but not below freezing, but the mother's face was red and raw.

She held a baby in her left arm and held the hand of a small boy on her right. He had pulled the draw string of his red Georgia sweatshirt tight.

"You must be Ms. Morris," I said, having been prompted by my co-worker. "You already know you belong in room number three, right?"

"We know where we belong, and we know the drill." Not hostile, just tired.

Everyone got fed; clothes got washed; the new family got settled.

We volunteers divided the night. Two awake from ten to two; two awake from two to six. Everyone up at six for breakfast and church. Out by eight.

I took the two-to-five sleeping shift. I was surprised that I slept so hard. My head was fuzzy for the first part of our four-hour shift. We read; we whispered; we stared.

"I'm not so sure about the church service in the morning, Martha."

"Don't worry. It's short and sweet."

When the time came, I sort of got swept in with the crowd. Most of the families came. They weren't that eager to get on the street.

St. Bart's was a failed 1950s architectural experiment. The sanctuary was dark with a circle of light enveloping the altar. The altar was on a circular platform circumscribed by a black rail. All of us gathered around the rail. I stood just outside the light as if I wasn't ready to go through customs to the church world.

The priest came in and stood behind the altar. A short, bearded man. White vestment, purple stole.

I recognized the words, and I knew the responses. But I couldn't say them. They were a language from another time. The priest talked about Jesus not giving up on anyone. I didn't know what he was talking about. It sounded like a canned speech, a hard sell for these folks. *Easy for you to say when you got a car and home.* Of course, I conveniently ignored that I had a car and a home too.

When we said the Creed I stared at the floor. It felt like a time warp. Virgin Birth. Descended to the dead. *This is the 1980's, not the Middle Ages.*

Then he came around with the bread. Round wafers with a cross etched in the middle. The woman beside me whispered to her son, "Put your stuff down and hold out your hands together." He did and I did.

The priest put the wafer in my hands and said, "The Body of Christ, the bread of heaven," and tears came down my face. I took an intake of breath. I couldn't remember weeping since I saw *Lassie.* I put the wafer in my mouth. The last time I had taken communion, the wafers melted, but these had to be chewed.

I wept. No noise, but tears running down my face. I wiped them with my sleeve, but they didn't stop. I took a step back to get farther in the dark. I had no idea what was happening to me. It seemed that a plug was pulled, and all my defenses fell down.

When the chalice bearer came to me with the chalice of wine, I reached for it with my right hand to guide it to my mouth—as I had been properly taught as a child—but my hand was shaking so badly I had to let go.

She guided it to my lips and said, "The blood of Christ, the cup of salvation."

Was it? Is this what this was about? Heaven and salvation? Even with all my Emory graduate classes in religion, I didn't know what that meant. I only knew that something was happening to me.

When the service was over, I bolted for the door, but the guests blockaded the exit—kids getting their coats, parents finding their bus tokens, the everydayness. Martha grabbed my arm. "See you next week, okay?"

I was back in control but not up for explanations.

"Okay." And then I left.

The next week I ate the bread and drank the wine and wept. And the next week and the next.

I didn't want to talk to the priest. I knew it would go downhill because the words didn't make sense. I dealt with words every day in graduate school, but this was too big. It was beyond the safety of academia with its carefully footnoted analyses. My worlds were divided—a dissertation about poems describing mystical experiences and wafers that had to be chewed. I couldn't bridge the gap. To avoid conversation at the end of each church service, I walked as quickly as I could into the crisp Atlanta morning.

But I went back again and again. I couldn't make sense of anything, but I had found a hunger that only that little wafer could feed.

Maybe it was nostalgia. Maybe it was a way to get back to some idealized childhood I craved but never lived. But maybe I was tired of reading about people connected to God while I felt empty inside.

After three weeks, Jo said, "So. Is this a church thing or a shelter thing? Are you easing in the back door?"

"I don't know what I am doing," I said. "But I am going back this Thursday."

The first time I went to a Sunday service, the assistant rector preached. I didn't like his voice. It was reedy. His sermon was on Christianity as the only way to salvation. I shed no tears that day. I left the church during the last hymn.

When I got home I wrote him a three-page, single-spaced letter. I quoted Martin Buber and *The Cloud of Unknowing*. My letter ended with "The God that can be put in a box isn't God."

The next Thursday, the rector caught up with me after communion. He patted my shoulder as if we were longtime friends. He cocked his head and said with a half laugh, "My assistant says you teed off on him. Is that right?"

I was glad it was dark so he couldn't see me blush. "Well, we had a difference of opinion."

"Yep," he said, "sounds like The Episcopal Church to me."

* * *

In the next three years, I moved from the shadows into the lighted circle. Soon I was a reader in church and played on the softball team. William James said, ". . . so the art of being wise is the art of knowing what to overlook."[1] I then was more than wise. I didn't think too much about the bureaucracy or the finances. I was there for bread and wine, the shelter, the

1. James, *Principles of Psychology*, 369.

rector's sermons. I stopped writing the assistant. I didn't socialize. I didn't run for any office. I simply went to church—every Sunday and every Thursday morning because I wanted to be fed.

Just as I settled in, even taught a course on mysticism, we moved.

I received a Fulbright scholarship, and we spent a year in Portugal.

\* \* \*

We didn't return to Atlanta. In 1984 we moved to Nashville, Tennessee. I had a job teaching American Literature at Belmont College, a small Southern Baptist college. We bought a house close to the college. Jo worked for the Vanderbilt School of Medicine and our son, Arthur, went to Vanderbilt Day Care. We met some friends. We had a routine. Our life worked.

I liked teaching. I liked my colleagues. I taught Freshman English and also had an opportunity to teach a course on Thoreau, Emerson, Hawthorne, and Melville.

One spring afternoon, my Introduction to Literature Class was half over when I noticed the students were restless and unengaged. I had been talking about poetic structure—villanelles and sonnets and sestinas—but apparently I was the only one who cared.

"Let's look at a different kind of poem," I said. I asked the closest student to read a poem by Edna St. Vincent Millay.

The student was a petite eighteen-year-old who wrote exquisite essays but never said a word in class. She sat straight in her chair, her long brown hair in a ponytail. Her voice was clear and surprisingly strong as she began:

*I am not resigned to the shutting away of loving hearts in the hard ground*
*So it is, and so it will be, for so it has been, time out of mind:*
*Into the darkness they go, the wise and the lovely. Crowned*
*With lilies and with laurel they go; but I am not resigned.*

Her voice got softer. I could barely hear the last verse.

*Down, down, down into the darkness of the grave*
*Gently they go, the beautiful, the tender, the kind;*
*Quietly they go, the intelligent, the witty, the brave.*
*I know. But I do not approve. And I am not resigned.*[2]

She stared at her book and the class stared at her.

"What's going on?" I asked. "What does this say to you?"

2. Millay, "Dirge Without Music," 493.

She looked above my head as she answered. "So much happens. You tell yourself it can be different, but you know it won't. I know it won't. This poet may not be resigned," she said, now almost whispering. "But the dead are still dead."

"Yes," I said. "They are."

We sat for a few moments until I said, "Okay, that's enough for today." My student reader walked hurriedly along the back wall and out the door.

That day and other days like that day were clues that I was becoming more interested in the students than the subject. My heart went out to that student and my head forgot about Edna St. Vincent Millay.

* * *

In 1987 Jo and I were sitting on our porch swing. It was early spring and a Sunday afternoon. No bugs, no humidity. The iris leaves were up but the blooms had yet to come. Arthur was at a friend's house. I saw our neighbor working in her flower bed across the street and from the apartment house next door I heard the jazz program from the local Public Radio.

We had the *New York Times* between us. Jo was looking at the Arts and Leisure section, but I preferred reading the wedding announcements on the Styles page. What were the criteria for getting included? I wondered.

I could hear the phone ringing in the kitchen and almost let it go.

"Bam? It's Mom."

Her voice was high pitched—a signal something was wrong.

"It's about your dad," she said. "You know we've been worried about his kidneys." This was a piece of knowledge I had discarded. The distance between me and my father was filled with too many land mines for me to hold him in my daily consciousness. Sometimes I thought of my past as if it were someone else's narrative I could analyze from my safe academic space. I knew my father had lost most of his sight. I knew that he could only hear the television when it was blasting, but I did not carry that knowledge anywhere near my heart.

"What about his kidneys?"

"They shut down. He'll have to be on dialysis." My mother sounded small as if she were in retreat.

"I'm so sorry, Mom. What can I do?"

"Come and see him. He misses you. It's been too long."

"Mom, I'll do my best."

When I walked back to the porch, I wasn't just thinking about my dad. I wasn't just thinking about the kind of son I had become or my regrets over all that hadn't been.

I was thinking about time. For the first time I realized that if my dad was going to die, I would eventually die too. I realized that my time, like his, was limited and it came to me clearly: *You had better move to be a priest. Now.* I didn't know how. I didn't know if I could do it, but I knew this mattered to me and that mattering outweighed all my doubts about not being good enough or smart enough, and even outweighed my fears of being part of the church. I realized my life in limbo over this had to be over—whatever happened. In or out.

I sat next to Jo and told her about my father. She asked me a lot of medical questions I couldn't answer.

"You know this is the beginning of the end, don't you?" she said.

I nodded and we swung back and forth.

"Jo," I said. I didn't look at her but straight ahead at the next-door apartment building. "I can't explain this, but I want to look into being a priest."

For a while we swung.

"Is this connected to your dad?"

"Probably. Yes. I'm scared of time running out."

"Well," she said. "Either do it or don't, but you need to figure this out once and for all."

\* \* \*

For a year I was part of a group of "aspirants"—people who want to go to seminary and be ordained. There were eight of us—all men, even though The Episcopal Church had been ordaining women since 1976. I didn't know anyone.

The leader was the priest from a small blue-collar parish on the southern edge of Nashville. We met one evening a month at his parish in one of the Sunday School rooms. We sat in a circle on metal folding chairs. I always brought a thermos of coffee to make it through the two hours. Each week he'd give us a topic and we were to bring a "Reflection"— a two-page meditation—which we read aloud.

The first night, the bishop came. He was tall and had a patrician demeanor. With his white wavy hair, he looked like a foreign ambassador.

I found it hard to talk to him. He didn't care enough to keep up a conversation or ask about any of us.

"There are two things I want to tell you," he said. "First, you need to be open here. The Chair needs to know who you are. So don't hold back and don't tell us what you think we want to hear." Then he said, "But the truth is, we can't place all the people who want to be priests. So, my guess is that one of you will be sent along. We don't have a quota, but we can only place one person a year."

"Okay," I thought. "We are going to be open as long as we say things that will make us look good?"

In the end, the group got along. We read our reflections. The facilitator had us talk about baptism and the eucharist and evangelism and forgiveness. None of us cried or talked about our dysfunctional families, and it wasn't anywhere near armed combat.

But I was never clear about the criteria. I thought the frontrunner was the youth minister at the charismatic Episcopal Church in town. He was younger than me and grew up Baptist. Therefore, he had a Bible quote for every circumstance. When it was his time to pray, he always bowed his head and held out both hands in supplication. He waited long enough for me to get itchy and sometimes started prayer with "I just want to thank God for…"

Because he was nice and kind and sincere, he didn't trigger my academic stance of superiority. I had little in common with him, but I liked him. In response to the facilitator's questions, he began with Bible quotes but then added examples from his church experience, while all I had was Rainer Maria Rilke quotes. I thought the guy would make a good priest.

The others seemed less focused. The truth is we were all going through midlife crises. Most of us were past thirty-five. A few were in their fifties. Clearly something had happened to all of us that made us change directions.

To my surprise, we didn't talk much about our families. The priest at our home church in Nashville, told me, "All you have to do is cry and get angry and you'll pass. Tell them you have issues with your mother and you're working on your identity, and you'll be fine."

"What about Jesus and what about all my doubts about whether the Bible is accurate?" I asked him.

"What do you mean?"

"I mean that most of it is myth—Red Sea, Burning Bush, Ten Commandments. What if they ask me if it's true?"

"Number one. They won't ask you. We're Episcopalians. Number Two. Tell the truth, whatever they ask."

It didn't come up.

What did come up was pushing us about our call. Near the last of our sessions, the facilitator talked about calling. He read the Bible passages about Samuel, and Moses, and Jeremiah being called, and then he turned to the group. "Tell us why you think you are called to be a priest."

None of us gave a great response. Most people talked about the importance of the Eucharist. The evangelical aspirant said, "I have been pastoring people unofficially as a youth worker. I'd like to be more intentional about it."

When it was my turn, I didn't know what to say so I started talking. "I have wanted to be a priest since I was six, but I don't know if I can say why. I think I want my life to matter and serving God seems like the most important thing. I know from teaching that I like to talk in public." I paused to think. "It's the mattering thing. The church ought to be about people's lives and connecting those lives to the source. I'd like to be part of that."

I couldn't tell if that was the worst answer or the best. We all kind of looked at each other until the facilitator said what a great group we had and how honored he was to be part of it.

The priest said, "I will report to the bishop, and he'll get in touch with you."

* * *

On a spring Saturday in 1989 a cream-colored envelope landed in our mailbox. I was in the yard looking at the grass to see if I could postpone mowing for another week. Jo came out with the letter held away from her body like an offering. "It's time to see which road you're on," she said. I saw on the top left corner the words: "The Office of the Bishop."

For a moment I couldn't breathe. I looked at Jo and slowly shook my head back and forth. "I don't know," I said.

She kissed me on the cheek. "I don't either, but I know I love you and I know you'll still be you regardless of what that letter says."

"Here goes," I said, and tore back the flap and pulled out the cream-colored stationary.

It was short. Two sentences. "This letter is to inform you that I grant you postulancy for the priesthood in The Episcopal Church. Please contact my Assistant for an appointment to discuss this."

"What does it say?" Jo asked.

"Yes. It says yes."

"Oh, Bam." She grabbed me and held me.

When we got inside the house, she asked, "How do you feel?"

"Excited and a little scared," I said, and turned to her. "What about you? How is this for you?"

"I am very scared and a little excited because it's going to turn our lives around."

I looked at her for a moment and then asked, "In a good way?"

"Well," she said, "in every way." Then she said, "What's next?"

# 3

# Seminary at Sewanee

If God were small enough to be understood, He would not be big enough to be worshipped.

—EVELYN UNDERHILL, *THE SPIRITUAL LIFE*

"THERE'S NOWHERE TO GO here."

My seven-year-old son, Arthur, said this as a proclamation—as if he had discovered an eternal truth.

"Arthur, this is our first day," I said. "There are plenty of places to go. This is going to be the best year of your life. You'll see."

Even I didn't believe that. We were standing on the Main Street of Sewanee, Tennessee, in August of 1991. A team of movers had just stuffed our belongings into a matchbox house on South Carolina Avenue. My going to seminary meant that our family of four moved from our spacious 3000 square-foot house in Nashville to a 1000 square-foot house in Sewanee. Our daughter Marie's room was so small that two people couldn't fit side to side next to her crib.

"Don't worry," I told the kids. "There are woods and trails, and you'll have hundreds of friends. It will be like a two-year camp."

It was the first of August and there we stood on University Avenue. School began in three weeks, but the town looked like *The Day After*. Arthur started running in circles. Marie being three years old, started jumping up and down in her stroller and loudly commanding Jo, "Let's go Mommy." So, Jo rolled her up the street away from the darkened store.

Sewanee is the town the world forgot. Twelve hundred residents and twelve hundred students and a campus with a faux Oxford look on top of a ridge overlooking the Tennessee plain. There are reasons its proper name is The University of the South. Nothing changes quickly. And it was still a world where white men were in charge.

When we went into the University Chapel, Arthur pointed to the ceiling. "Look at the flags."

Hanging down the main aisle were the flags from the Confederate states—with Mississippi's Confederate St. Andrew's Cross fluttering.

Jo looked at me. "Are you sure about this? It's a long way from your taking those classes at Vanderbilt Divinity last year."

"No," I said. "I am not sure, but it's the hoop we have to jump through."

* * *

Ten months earlier, in October of 1989, I met the bishop in his office in a Victorian house on the edge of downtown Nashville. The bishop was in his early sixties—tall, white hair, pudgy face, and a high voice. That was my first real encounter with him. I sat in a straight back chair, wearing my dark gray suit. He sat on a low leather sofa, wearing his traditional purple shirt. For reasons I never understood at that point in my life, the bishop had a bag of popcorn on his lap. His comments were spaced between fistfuls of white kernels going into his mouth.

"Bishop," I said in a voice of supplication. "Thank you for approving me for seminary. Because I have lived in the South all my life, I wondered if you'd allow me to go to an Episcopal seminary in a different region—like General in New York or VTS in Washington or Seabury in Chicago or CDSP in Berkeley?"

He looked at me as if I were a willful child. "No. You are going to Sewanee."

"Okay," I said, and took a breath to calm down. "You're the bishop." We stared at each other while I considered an alternative.

"How about this? Since my wife has a job at Vanderbilt and my two kids are happy in school and daycare, is it okay if I commute? It's only an hour and a half from Nashville to Sewanee."

"No." Crunch. "You are living there. Sewanee's about the whole experience of being on the Mountain."

Long silence. "Bishop," I said in a low tight voice, trying to quell my anger, "this is about obedience, right?"

He looked at me, cocked his head and almost smiled. "Right. It is."

* * *

So here we were at our new home. Sewanee.

"This is the deadest place I've ever seen," Arthur said.

At my son's proclamation I looked across the street at the bookstore with its red-letter "CLOSED" sign framed by dark glass. No one walking on the street. No dogs loitering. No cars obeying the 25-mile-an-hour speed limit or any limits. Just the hot August afternoon and a stillness that was more about absence than possibility.

We walked down the street and came to the local Episcopal Church. Behind the dark stone church was a playground and a low flat-roof building that looked like a 1950s motel. "I need to go to the bathroom," Arthur declared. He and I went into this new building, and to our surprise discovered that the second room on the right was filled with books. Behind the desk was an elderly lady maybe early seventies—her gray hair in a bun. She wore black no-nonsense shoes.

"We're new here," I said. "This is Arthur, and my name is Bam Taylor."

I was surprised at how quickly she moved. Trink Beasley shook my hand formally and said in a strong Midwestern voice, "I am so glad to meet you. You and your son must come to my house for lunch. We're having pizza."

Arthur jumped up and down. "Great," he said. "Pizza is my favorite."

"We'd love to." I was relieved to meet someone—anyone.

It turned out that she and her husband lived next door to us, and they became our salvation. They became grandparents to our children. They introduced us to townspeople. They fed us when we ran out of money and food and they lifted our spirits when we forgot why we had moved to this nowhere mountain.

The pizza we ate that day was the bread that almost erased my trepidation about what we had done by coming here.

But when Jo and I lay in our beds that night, I felt a wave of second thoughts. I was reading *Father Melancholy's Daughter* by Gail Godwin. Jo was knitting a sweater.

"I'm sorry I dragged you here. I know it sucks for you. You've got a three-hour round trip commute to Vanderbilt. And God knows who we will talk to. I wish I knew another way."

She put her knitting down and turned to me. "I can't pretend I like being here. It's like a combination of Peyton Place and Mayberry, but I love you. So, if we need to be here, we need to be here." She went back to her knitting.

"Thank you," I said.

"You're welcome but don't forget. You owe me, and I mean big time."

\* \* \*

I walked into the chapel, but I had to look down not up. The room was a converted chemistry lecture hall with seats descending. I didn't think about where to sit. I certainly didn't realize this decision would fix me in that chair for two years. I found a seat at the top so I could lean my head against a wall, and so no one would look at me. For all my talk about being called, I felt as if I were in the third grade. Would anyone sit next to me? Talk to me? Would they find out about my doubts? How I didn't believe the Red Sea parted or Jesus walked on the water, or Mary got pregnant by the Holy Spirit? Was I too standoffish for this crowd?

"Breathe," I told myself. "You've waited your whole life for this."

Because I closed my eyes, I felt, not saw, someone sit next to me.

When I turned, he grabbed my hand. "Welcome to the Pit—that's our name for the chapel. The good news is, if you can find Jesus here, you can find him anywhere."

He laughed a long high laugh and something in me loosened. "Hey," he said. "You're in luck. The preacher today actually has something to say."

At the end of the service, we filed out to go to lunch. As I walked with the crowd, I could hear loud voices in the hallway. An argument. A loud argument.

A faculty member, who looked like an ecclesial Falstaff—obese, red faced—was shoving his index finger into the chest of a fellow professor who was one third the aggressor's weight. This second man's white hair looked as if he had serious static cling.

The angry man shouted in a baritone voice, "I'll break the bread any way I want to. You are an outdated academic."

His adversary was at least six inches shorter and looked like William Faulkner. His voice was slow. When he held up his hands in defense, I could see the yellow nicotine marks on his fingers.

"No one can change the rubrics in The Prayer Book. The rubrics are our rules and they're there for a reason, and it's to keep order." His face was tight—squinched in anger. "Do you even know the rules?"

Seminarians formed a circle as if we were in an elementary school playground. But then a short bald-headed professor jumped into the circle, grabbed the smaller man's arm, and led him through the crowd as he gave instructions in his ear.

"Welcome to Sewanee," my new friend said. "It's usually pretty boring but it always has the potential of being squirrely. It's what happens when you're on a godforsaken mountain for three years."

That day I knew he and I would be friends, and I knew this place was not completely safe. I had come out of academia, and I knew its pettiness. I wanted no part of it. I was desperate to believe in the church and what I was trying to become. My main question was not about Jesus or God or salvation. It wasn't about the Bible either. I knew scripture was more of a road map than an historical record. My question was representing the institution of the Church with its flaws and shadows. My twin sister had asked the North Carolina bishop in 1972 if she could be a priest. She was turned down because she wasn't a male. I didn't want to represent a white male country club church—much less one that argued over breaking the bread in the Eucharist.

"What the hell was that about?" I asked my friend.

"You mean the match between the two professors?"

"And we're supposed to learn what about leadership and community from that?"

"As I said before, welcome to Sewanee."

\* \* \*

The School of Theology began the semester the way Sewanee began everything: booze and conversation. The dean sponsored a cocktail party the night before classes began. I clutched my soda water as I held Jo's hand. We stood like the couple in the Amish painting. Looking at the crowd, I tried to pick out the new students from the old, but I wasn't sure who was who. The clue was the level of anxiety. Those of us who were anxious about this new thing either looked like a plant—that would be me—or they looked as if they were deejaying the party. They either didn't try or tried way too hard. Truthfully, I wasn't standoffish out of any judgment, but I just didn't know what to say. "So, what do you do about your doubts about the church?" or "How do you deal with the fact that even though you show up for prayer every day, God always seems to have something better to do than visit you?" Being a plant was safer.

But nothing was safe with the woman who came and stood in front of me beyond my comfort zone. "Hey, you must be Bam Taylor," she said so loudly in my ear that I flinched. "I've heard about you. You're the professor, right?"

I took a step back and nodded. Jo moved a step away.

"I hear you're spiritual. Is that right?"

"Well, I don't know about that. I've read a lot of Thomas Merton and I go on retreats to the Monastery. Is that spiritual?"

"It is for me. Listen. You need to get into Cursillo. Now. That's where the real Spirit is. It's no good to be silent. God works with movement and energy." She leaned into me, her head almost touching mine. "I am going to make this happen for you." She squeezed my arm as she walked away.

I looked to see Jo with her back to me, now talking to another woman. I walked over and Jo introduced me. She said, "I saw you talking to your fellow seminarian. I'll bet she talked about Cursillo. You need to remember one thing. That woman doesn't make friends. She takes prisoners."

* * *

When I walked into the middler (second year) classroom for my first class at Sewanee, I was back in junior high. I hadn't realized that I would take all my classes in this one room. Seminarians didn't go to the professor's room; the professors came to the seminarians. I was in junior high because I realized that whoever I sat next to, I would be next to that person every day for the year in the middler classroom.

About half the class was present. I knew none of them. The guy I'd met at the cocktail party was nowhere to be seen. I wished for some theological indicators. Perhaps we could be color coded, just like political parties—red for any literalists, blue for those who think the Bible is sheer myth, orange for social activists, and so forth. How do you know what someone thinks and how they behave based on how they look?

I took a step in. On the front row sat a short woman, perhaps a little older than me. She wore a black dress that marked her as a professional person in my eyes. And she looked fun.

"Hi. I'm Bam Taylor. Can I sit next to you for the next nine months?"

"Sure you can. I'm from New Orleans, so as long as you celebrate Mardi Gras and don't root against the Saints, you are welcome right here."

Something in me released. Maybe this would be okay. I didn't expect lifelong friends. I had two children and a wife who was working too hard and my whole other issues. I was sober for a year but had been to only one AA meeting here. I didn't want to be a stranger in a strange land.

And more. To believe in this church, I needed to believe in these people and in my capacity to be real with them. Because I knew that it was an illusion to think there was a church that was infected with all kinds of limitations and toxic syndromes and somehow in our sanitized seminary we were going to analyze their issues so we could save them. I had given that up in academia. There is no ivory tower and no seminary sanctuary. There's just us. All of us. The church out there was in this classroom and if I was going to give my life to it, I needed to feel that regardless of beliefs or practices, people had good intentions, good will, and deep hearts. Otherwise, we were all wasting our time.

My two new acquaintances were breadcrumbs that pointed to a hope beyond my dark wood of doubts.

* * *

My first months of seminary went well. I discovered that good writing covers a multitude of ignorance. The classes were not terribly hard but only a few were provocative or very imaginative. I took the standard courses: Church History, Liturgics (Worship), Old and New Testament, Homiletics (Preaching), Pastoral Care, and Ethics. Mainly it involved listening to talking heads. The professors talked and we wrote down what they said.

Homiletics was where everything became real for me. I liked Homiletics because we got to hear one another's sermons and offer critique. It was more than that. I loved preaching because I lost myself in the words and when I preached, I felt more connected with the people in the room. There was an energy circuit that bonded us together.

My first day of preaching in chapel came in my second semester. Instead of being perched in my last-row seat, I stood at the pulpit looking up into the sea of faces that reminded me both of Dante's Celestial Rose and the Roman Pantheon—maybe more of the latter than the former.

"When I came home from Grace Elementary School, Anna, our maid, and my sister and I would go to our den and watch *Queen for a Day*. Sally and I would sit while Anna stood ironing clothes."

That's how I began. When I spoke those words, I could see my classmates focus and perk up. Jesus and *Queen for a Day*?

I talked about my childhood excitement over the contestant winning a washing machine, only to be scolded by Anna who said, "How is that washing machine going to help that woman feed her kids?" I ended with, "If the

Gospel is good news, it's got to be more than giving washing machines. It's got to give hope for a new world."

Sermons were the only consistent place I found to play. Seminary was earnest and sincere but deadly serious. So many assignments in other classes reminded me of writing reports in my youth by finding some experts to quote. Sermons didn't follow those rules. They had different rules: be honest, go deep, open yourself up.

There was one other dimension. Because sermons were one step removed from my raw feelings that I kept so protected, preaching allowed me to get closer to telling the truth about what was really going on inside me. The pulpit became a safe container to come clean.

When I preached about the Prodigal Son, I mined my biographical wounds without naming them. "The younger son didn't leave because of his sudden fortune. He wasn't looking for a good time. He just didn't know how much his father loved him. So, he left to test it. As he walked toward the distant country, he kept hoping his daddy would call him back. And because there was no call, he went as far as he could go—a pigsty in the middle of nowhere."

I didn't have to say, "That's me. That's my story." But because it was, the energy circuit simply contained more. I felt myself drawn to what Yeats called "the rag-and-bone shop of the heart" even though I knew not everyone shared this thirst for intensity. That's not why some people, maybe many people, come to church.

I worried that I cared too much about my sermons. I worried that it was my ecclesial version of trying to be a rock star. But my worries could not stop my focus on them.

Because our house was so small and because I wanted to see my children at the end of the day, I did little work at night except to read in bed as Jo read her mystery novels. Instead, I set my alarm for 4:30 a.m. and drove to a long wooden barracks built when Sewanee had a military academy. The bedrooms were now student studies. I'd take a thermos of coffee and work until 7:00. In that stillness sometimes, many times, the words came.

\* \* \*

Seminary was all about information and to some degree imitation. We grasped data and we practiced a different routine of life: Morning Prayer every day at 8:30 a.m., weekly Eucharist Wednesday at noon, Friday evening, and Sunday morning. To my astonishment our training was about our heads and our feet—what we thought and where we showed up, but it wasn't much about our hearts.

One morning I learned how dangerous that was. I was sitting on the back row of Chapel. A student in her forties was conducting the service. I thought she was sweet, sincere. She had several children ages three to eight. I knew she was married, but I never learned her husband's name.

Her work study was to organize worship services for the undergraduate students in the University Church. She would come in and tell us about the crazy college kids.

That morning she processed in, donned in her long black-and-white robes that covered everything but her face and long brown wavy hair. When she stood at her place under the cross, I heard a voice in my head saying, "She looks as if she is being crucified." She didn't say anything. She didn't make any gesture. No tears. But she appeared to be in agony.

I wrote her a letter that morning telling her what I thought was happening and saying if it were true, I'd help anyway I could.

No word from her, but two weeks later she left school and her family and the mountain. Though I wasn't sure why, my thoughts were clear. *The problem isn't the instruction at the seminary. The problem is that if you don't deal with your insides, of course, you'll explode. And Sewanee is not getting anywhere near that.*

\* \* \*

The loser from the move to Sewanee was Jo. Tenfold. The kids loved being there. It was like living in *The Donna Reed Show*. Kids and dogs were everywhere. My favorite part of the day was going to the Sewanee Elementary School at 3:30. All the parents gathered on the sidewalk waiting for their kids. At 3:15 one of the two Sewanee police showed up, his blue light circling on top of his car. He was there to protect and defend, even though there were few cars going back and forth.

The bell would ring and out came the flow of kids. I'd rustle Arthur's hair and we'd cross the street to get Marie out of the church daycare. We'd walk to our little house and play with the dog, or the kids would go into the "fort" they built in the woods, or we'd build a fire in the fireplace and roast marshmallows. We couldn't afford cable TV, so we had to entertain ourselves.

Arthur had a handful of buddies from the elementary school. Some afternoons he'd disappear on his bicycle. Or he'd ask me for two dollars for his walk up to the Campus Store to get a drink and chips. He knew this place was a safe container and he relaxed into being an eight-year-old boy.

Marie loved her daycare teacher as much as she did me. Plus, the teacher's son was a towhead her same age. At three years old Marie didn't remember much of Nashville or know what to miss.

I had Seminary with all its warts and wonders. But Jo only had her job back in Nashville. Three days a week she drove ninety minutes there and ninety minutes back. Her last twenty miles were up the mountain which was always fogged in from December to March. We bought a Honda Civic knowing she would wear it out.

When she came home, she was too tired for any Seminary suppers, much less a Seminarian's Spouses Group.

"Here's the deal," she told me one night as we lay in bed reading. "You three have a life here. You have friends and you're busy. But all I have here is the three of you. My life is in Nashville. Plus, let's face it. Half the people here are really strange."

"Only half?" I asked.

She turned and looked at me. "Look. We're doing this because you need to. But there's a toll. There's a really big toll."

"I know and you're the main one whose paying it. Right?"

"Right. Really right."

* * *

I asked my pastoral theology professor if he would be my Spiritual Director. He came to Sewanee after being a rector of a large church in Pennsylvania. Tall, lanky, unassuming. He had two verbal oddities. His laugh was a loud cackle and he stuttered. But when everyone else was on the surface, Charles was always holding the door of the elevator open to go down deep.

"So Bam, let's start with how you pray. Tell me about your prayer life."

We sat in his living room with its view of the woods through the long plate glass window. We faced each other in leather chairs. I stared at the woods looking for a suitable response.

"Well, I make a list of people to pray for and I offer them up in the morning. And I say a shortened version of Evening Prayer at night."

"And?"

"And. There is no and."

He looked at me with an uncomfortable directness. "Tell me how you experience God."

"Experience" was not a word I knew. I could tell him what theologians said about God. I could tell him of the famous mystics' experiences of God, but I hadn't had an experience of God since my trip to India and Assisi years ago.

"Well. God is God," I tried. "And so, all our experience is limited."

"Okay, Bam. I know you can think, but I am not asking you what you have read. I am asking what you know."

I looked again into the woods, and we sat.

Finally, I shook my head. "I want to know God. I don't want to be a fraud as a priest, and I feel hollow inside. Mostly I long to know God, but I don't know where to start."

"You just did. It's the wanting that matters and it's setting aside time for the One who wants you. Pray twenty minutes in silence every morning, every day. No books, no music, just one on one. You and God." And then Charles added, "Use The Second Song of Isaiah before you start."

I wanted to ask what that was, but I pretended to know. "Good choice," I said. When I got home I discovered it's the passage that begins "Seek the Lord while he wills to be found; call upon him when he draws near."

As we got to the door, he said, "Remember Bam. This is the one place where words are not your friend. This isn't about your doing anything but showing up."

The next morning, in my little study room in the barracks, I sat still for twenty minutes, but I wouldn't call it prayer. I thought of things undone—projects, kids' events, papers. I kept looking at my watch. I didn't do much better the next day or the next week.

But slowly, after showing up day after day, some stillness came. I sat in my chair, feet on the ground, eyes closed, and I breathed in and said in my head "Lord Jesus Christ have mercy on me" and I breathed out and said in my head "a sinner." Again and again. Breath by breath. This repetition was like a fan that waved the mosquito thoughts away.

I never got the voice from Mount Sinai, but a peaceful stillness, a place where my critical voices took a break. Sometimes I experienced a sense of rightness or calm assurance, a connectedness and coherence. It was as if I knew there was a ground floor to this life or a solid place to stand. I didn't know if this was a religious experience, but it helped to balance all the words in the classroom and assured me that my journey wasn't limited to my head. It didn't guarantee that I would not go off the rails like the female seminarian, but at least for one period in the day my demons sat in the corner and were mostly quiet. And I felt less like a fraud talking about God.

Of course, I never talked about this at the Seminary because it never came up in our serious intellectual inquiries.

* * *

I learned a lot about being a priest my first year at Sewanee. I learned about preaching and pastoral care. I learned about how the New Testament was put together. It was uncomfortable for me to learn that there was no surviving manuscript of any of the gospels. The word was "redacted" which sounded a whole lot like "made up," but I learned to deal with that. I learned about preaching and ethics and theology.

But most of all, I learned that if I was going to serve the church, I had to learn that it wasn't my church and it wasn't my world. And I learned that I knew so little about anything I thought I knew.

In the row behind me in class, sat a short, overweight and, I thought, overaged man. He was from Idaho and was in his late fifties. He had a buzz flat top, which I thought kind of marked him for being out of step with what was really going on. He had been in home insurance before coming here. He always wore long sleeve button-down shirts.

He seldom asked questions. When he gave a report, I was always bored.

In October of that year, at the end of ethics class, he raised his right hand to be recognized. "I have to tell you something. I have melanoma. It's my left arm. And it's bad."

He finished that semester but missed most of our classes in January. He came back in February. His face was a creamy sickly color. His left arm had been amputated. When he returned, he said, "I am not really here for my education. I am here for yours. You need to do more than talk about being pastors. Look at me and you see what lies before you. I am in pain, just like the people in the pews will be."

A month later he died in Egleston Hospital in Chattanooga.

His funeral was at the University Chapel. Charles DuBois climbed up the stairs to the pulpit and in his stuttering, high-pitch voice, this is what he said:

"Faithfulness is not about being smart. It's not about being right about all the hot-button issues. It's not about the silly shirts and vestments the priests wear. Our brother didn't care about any of those things. He wasn't the smartest student. He wasn't a good preacher. He didn't keep up with the Episcopal turmoil.

But he loved the Lord and he loved the church and he wanted to dedicate his life to making a difference for ordinary people living ordinary lives and trying to find their way. And he wasn't afraid to live the life given to him. And that's good. And that's worthy of all of our callings. My prayer for you is that you can be like him."

Sitting in my pew, I forgot for a moment about my doubts about myself and the seminary and the church. I let go of my fears of how any of this would turn out and I let go of my fear of ruining my family's life by dragging them here.

I simply wanted to be faithful—in that quiet, certain way like the man we just buried.

# 4

## The Move

I was free. I had recovered my liberty. I belonged to God, not to myself, and
to belong to Him is to be free, free of all the anxieties and worries and sorrow
that belong to this earth . . . What was the difference between one place and
another, one habit and another, if your life belonged to God.

—THOMAS MERTON, THE SEVEN STOREY MOUNTAIN

I CAN'T BELIEVE IT'S *this small.* This was my thought as I stood behind
the altar of St. Gregory the Great Episcopal Church. Jo and I had come to
Athens, Georgia, so I could be interviewed by the Vestry. They were trying
to decide if they wanted me to be their rector. I had come thinking this was
the right fit, but that was before I saw the church.

First, the church was a box—and a small, tall box at that. My guess was
it fit about 150 people. It looked like someone's living room: sliding glass
doors on both side walls and well-worn orange carpet, vintage 1975, but
with a twenty-five-foot arced ceiling. Maybe I could have overlooked the
floor and doors, but not the mural that filled the back wall. Four figures on
each side of the door—I assumed Old and New Testament saints. Men on
one side and women on the other, about four feet tall. I kept looking at St.
Jerome because his face looked just like Richard Dreyfus. Across from him
was a female saint wearing a bright blue dress, hugging a unicorn. Where
was that in the Bible? The middle had a large cross, with about a six-foot
radius with a lion, ox, eagle, and man in each quadrant. I was guessing the

four gospels and had no clue which was which. I actually liked the painting, but it overwhelmed the space.

A pleasant sixty-year-old white-haired woman stood next to me. She was the senior warden, which meant her job was to sell me on the parish. I could smell the same lavender powder my mother used. A transplant from Wisconsin, she had a business-like approach. "Of course, we are small. But we are looking for someone with energy who can help us grow." She paused and looked me in the face. "Like you."

I did not return her gaze. "Could you give me a minute here?" When she didn't move, I added, "Alone?"

By myself I closed my eyes and breathed slowly in and out, repeating an ancient prayer that sometimes helped me feel centered, "Lord Jesus Christ have mercy on me a sinner." After ten or twelve repetitions, I opened my eyes, trying to imagine being the priest here. I had hoped for a laid-back, unpretentious, creative place, but this seemed over the line. Could I feel God's presence in a church with folding chairs and no pews? Sliding glass doors instead of stained glass? Orange carpet instead of anything else?

I closed my eyes again. A thought came to me. *Church is about people, not buildings. People.*

I had been ordained for three years and was currently the assistant rector at a church outside Nashville. Jo had a great job at Vanderbilt. Our two kids were happy and we had a wonderful 1924 house in the city, with gardens and oak floors and a secret room for the kids.

But I was forty-six and restless. I was not good at being number two. As assistant rector I did what needed to be done. I liked the rector a lot and respected him. He was great at going to the hospital, but we seldom talked about the things I held dear: contemplative prayer or Dante or St. Teresa or Thomas Merton. So I was being supportive by being a chameleon. I was being the Pip for his Gladys Knight.

I wanted my own people. I wanted to set a course along different lines, my lines. Maybe it was pride and ego. I tried to resist it because of the disruption it would cause Jo and the kids, but I couldn't ignore the signs. The longer I stayed at the Nashville church, the less alive I felt. I kept hearing this voice that said, "Why I am doing this?"

"It's about people," I repeated as I looked at the empty folding chairs. When I looked at the mural, I repeated, "People."

I found Jo in the parish hall surround by a dozen Vestry members. I noticed that no one except the senior warden wore business attire, and she looked like she was dressed for a concert—straight navy-blue dress and white pearls. One man wore a tie and sweater, and another wore a blazer over an Oxford cloth shirt—standard college town attire. For dinner we had takeout Chinese: an assortment of five dishes, egg rolls, and hot and sour soup. I couldn't tell if that meant no one had time to cook or they forgot and ordered at the last minute.

I didn't take much food because I knew I'd have to talk, and I was too nervous to eat anyway. As we sat at the tables put together to form a square, Jo nudged my side with her elbow. "Go look at that print in front of us," she whispered. Apparently St. Gregory's made their parish hall available for local artists to show their work. On one of the side walls was a print in black and white. It was a circle of symbols that included a Christian cross, the Buddhist wheel, the Jewish Star of David, the Muslim moon and star, the Zoroastrian fire symbol, and some letters from an alphabet and religion I didn't recognize. In the middle was a message in ornate calligraphy that said, "Mastery in Servitude." It was the seal of Meher Baba, the Indian Master that Jo followed—the one whose house I went to see in Pune where I got my electric shock. I looked at the print and turned to look at Jo. She lifted her eyebrows and nodded her head as if to say, "Not bad for an Episcopal Church."

The interview was actually enjoyable. They told me their Christian Education classes were primarily "Christianity and": "Christianity and World Religions," "Christianity and Poetry," "Christianity and Contemporary Issues." I discovered that of the twelve people there, ten had PhDs. Their questions made me feel more at home.

"How do you feel about parishioners writing their own Prayers of the People?"

"We have a Community Thanksgiving Service with a liturgy we wrote—is that okay with you?"

"Every Sunday people bring canned food and put it under the altar for the homeless shelter. Then we deliver it that afternoon. We'd love to have you come with us to meet the guests. How would you feel about that?"

I kept saying "yes" and I kept laughing with them.

As Jo and I drove back to Nashville the next day, we agreed that the money would have to work. Our main concern was her job and the kids' school. Arthur was entering the seventh grade and Marie the second. Normally college towns have great public schools. However, I heard the public schools in the county weren't all that great and I wondered if it was because most of the property in this county was nontaxable.

* * *

We spent the next week talking about what to do. We got out newsprint and charted out pros and cons. The University of Georgia (UGA) had an art school which would be good for Jo. Living in a university town would be interesting. However, the public schools were a question mark. And there was no university medical center. All our conversations were "On the one hand . . . " and "But then . . . "

Early one morning before the sun was up, I was sitting in the breakfast room drinking coffee. I had already said my prayers and written in my journal. Jo came down and sat beside me. As it was dark, I could see our images reflected in the glass—me in my purple Sewanee T-shirt and Jo in her flowered pajama top. Her blonde hair hung to her shoulders. We looked younger than we were. The worries of the day had not descended upon us.

"What do you want to do?" Jo asked as she held her cup of peppermint tea. I didn't hear an agenda in her voice. I didn't think she wanted to go. She liked the house and her friends and her job. The kids were settled.

"If you want to go, we'll go. We can make it work." She didn't sound resigned. Surprisingly, her tone was almost flippant as if she were saying, "It's no big deal," but I knew it was a big deal. I had dragged us to Sewanee, Tennessee, five years before, and now I was threatening to drag us to Georgia.

"I don't know why I want to do this, but I do. The church building isn't spectacular, but I like the people. I think it would be fun. I think Athens would be fun. But I don't want to make you and the kids martyrs."

We held hands for a little while. As we looked out the window, the day dawned. Our reflections faded and we could see outside to Jo's garden filled with purple and white iris.

She kissed my cheek. "You'll have to dig up all my flowers," she whispered in my ear. "I don't go without them."

\* \* \*

Three days later I drove to Athens to talk to the Vestry about a contract and to look at the church one more time.

We sat again in the Parish Hall. This night we had lasagna—takeout from the local Italian restaurant. The Vestry's questions were more specific now that it seemed we were doing more than dating.

"How much vacation do you need?"

"We have a lot of shut ins. How often can you visit them?"

"Do you make calls to the county jail? One of our parishioners is there on a drug charge."

When there was a lull in the conversation, the junior warden spoke in a voice a little shrill and rushed. "What about me? If you come here, is there a place for me in this church as a lesbian?"

The circle of people looked at me as if they were in the huddle and I was the quarterback. "Of course, there's a place for you," I said. "This isn't my church. It's God's church."

I felt a collective sigh.

We agreed on the salary. We agreed on vacation and a sabbatical and insurance. We agreed on a start date and moving costs. When I signed the contract, someone popped a champagne bottle. We toasted our new beginning with plastic "How Bout Them Dawgs?" red cups—twelve filled with champagne and mine with ginger ale.

"To new beginnings."

That night I drove to the downtown Holiday Inn. I called Jo to check in with her and went straight to sleep. It was about ten o'clock.

At two o'clock in the morning I sat straight up and said aloud, "Holy shit. We are screwed."

I thought of my children going to a new school without any friends.

I thought of leaving the Nashville house with its ten-foot ceilings and our forty-two new storm windows.

I thought of Jo going to work in her white Vanderbilt lab coat with her name in blue stitching above her left pocket.

All the demons I had kept bottled up came out and danced in my head. I paced from the door to the window and back muttering, "I am such a loser."

I knew I would never get back to sleep, so I dressed and made some coffee in the small white coffee pot in the bathroom.

When I went downstairs, the woman behind the desk asked in a tentative voice, "Everything okay?" She was clearly a college student. Long black hair, green fingernail polish, and way too much makeup for two thirty in the morning.

"Fine. I just have to check out."

As I drove through the empty highways, I listened to my old Joan Baez cassette. I turned up the volume and tried to let the clarity of her voice quiet my mind. "A Hard Rain's Going to Fall" played over and over.

I got to Nashville at seven thirty. Standing in the driveway, I could see our bedroom light on but no lights on the first floor. Jo was up but not dressed.

I made coffee for me, tea for her, and sat looking out the breakfast room window at the iris.

"Whoa. What are you doing here? You're in Athens planning our new life."

When she saw my face, she took both my cheeks in her hands and kissed me on the forehead like a mother greeting her child after school. I wrapped my arms around her and buried my face in her hair, still smelling like strawberries from her shampoo. "What happened?"

"I made a mistake. I don't think we should go."

This began a conversation with an ever-widening circle of participants. I thought someone must have a solution, and if I just kept asking for it, the answer would find me. I talked to my therapist and my sister and my boss and my former coworkers at the college. I talked to our neighbors and other priests in Nashville.

I was caught in the middle of the river. I couldn't go back. I really didn't see anything new there. St. Paul's was comfortable and worked for the four of us, but I was treading water. And I couldn't get to the other side either because of the uncertainty. What if I was wrong? What if I was sacrificing Jo and the kids for my restlessness?

During the day I was in my problem-solving mode. "Problems have solutions," I kept saying to myself. "Let's think this through."

But at night, I couldn't think, and I couldn't sleep. All our bedrooms were on the second floor. Jo and I would put the kids to bed, and then I would roam the downstairs holding my pillow and dragging my blanket behind me.

I listened to talk radio with my earphones. After midnight all I could find was "Coast to Coast" with Art Bell—a very weird program about UFOs and extraterrestrials. One woman talked about how she had been taken captive, but she couldn't see the aliens because the light of their ship blinded her. Another said there was a federation of space aliens that were connecting with one another to save our planet. Art Bell, the host, had a deep baritone voice and tone that implied that all of this was as normal as talking about the weather.

Much of the night I sat staring at the breakfast room window which meant I stared at myself. I couldn't read and didn't want to wake anyone by turning on the TV. I drank Jo's peppermint tea. I ate the kids' cookies. I read the local paper, the *Tennessean*, over and over. I liked the obituaries because they took so long to finish.

During the day I went to work but mostly sat in my office.

On day four, Jo said, "You need to get yourself together. Who can help you?" Her tone told me her patience was ebbing. She stood in front of me in her white lab coat with her arms crossed. Before I could respond she said, "Don't say you don't know. Who has helped you in the past?"

Then I thought of my Pastoral Theology professor in seminary who was also a priest. In his mid-sixties, he was still at Sewanee. We traded Christmas cards but hadn't talked in about a year.

I called him. "I am a mess," I began, and the rest spilled out.

When I finally paused, I heard him sigh. The he spoke in his kind of reedy voice that sometimes jammed from his stutter.

"Well, well, well. Here you are at the crossroads. Been here before?"

"What? No, this is my first search. I have no idea how it's supposed to go."

"Bam. You know this isn't about the job, don't you?"

But I didn't know that at all. I said, "What are you trying to tell me?"

"Look. When I moved to Sewanee from New Jersey, the same thing happened to me. My wife kept saying there's no place in Sewanee to go, not even a grocery store, and to make it worse, we're trapped in a constant Southern cocktail party. I was convinced I had messed up."

"And?" I said as he stopped talking. "And?"

"And one day I took a walk in the Sewanee woods. As I walked, I opened up and breathed. And I heard God speaking to me—that's not an everyday occurrence, I can tell you. God said, "Why don't you come out and play?"

I didn't know what to say. I didn't say anything.

"Bam? Did you hear me?"

"Thank you. I think I got it."

I didn't know how this all would work, but I did know I couldn't stand still. I didn't know if my kids would find a school that worked for them, or if Jo would find a job, or if we would find a place to live. I didn't know if the church in Athens would love or hate me or how I'd feel about them. But I did know that I had been trying to color within the lines most of my life, and the need to get it right meant I was never free enough to play.

I found Jo weeding in her garden. Her face was red from bending over. As I came near, she took off her gloves and wiped her forehead with her sleeve.

She crooked her head to the left and raised her eyebrows in a questioning look.

I wrapped my arms around her and whispered in her ear, "How do you feel about going to Athens to play?"

"I am all in," she replied.

## POSTSCRIPT:

All my anxiety disappeared my first Sunday at St. Gregory. I realized these people didn't want a performer, and they certainly didn't want a mayor or sheriff. They wanted someone who was present and available to travel with them in their journey of faith. Plus, they had a gift of play, which I sorely lacked. In eight years, they taught me what community is, and they welcomed me as I am. There were many days as a bishop when I wondered why I left St. Gregory. Being with them was not only an honor; it was fun. Because of that, we as the whole parish accomplished more than I dreamed of.

# 5

# General Convention 2003

As long as we are on earth, the love that unites us will bring us suffering
by our very contact with one another because this love is the resetting
of a Body of broken bones.

—THOMAS MERTON, *NEW SEEDS OF CONTEMPLATION*


"NO TEARS FOR QUEERS."

That was the first sign I saw at General Convention 2003. I was walk-ing down the sidewalk leading to the Minneapolis Convention Center and saw a cluster of people standing across the street from the entrance, waving placards in the air. Next to "No tears for queers" was "Fags die. God laughs." In front of a dozen protestors was a skinny white man wearing a black suit and a tan cowboy hat. A large bullhorn hid his face.

As I neared the convention center I heard him say, "What happened to Sodom and Gomorrah will happen to The Episcopal Church. God sees your sin and God hates the sinful."

I followed the crowd. We veered to the right to get away from the bullhorn. The man shouted, "You can avoid me, but you cannot avoid the Judgment Day. God sees what you are doing."

I quickened my pace, stared at the ground, and wondered what I had gotten myself into. The woman next to me was almost jogging. Taking my longest strides, I asked her, "Who are these people?"

"That's some fanatic from Oklahoma. He drives all over the country to spread his bile."

"He's an Episcopalian?"

"Oh no. But you know this year, all the crazies will turn out."

Above the doorway was a blue sign with white letters: "The Episcopal Church Welcomes You."

\* \* \*

Every three years The Episcopal Church assembles for the General Convention to do the business of the church. Each of the 109 dioceses elects four clergy and four lay people as deputies to vote on resolutions ranging from authorizing new hymns to taking a position on the Israeli/Palestinian conflict. There are an additional one hundred plus bishops representing each diocese. It's said to be one of the largest religious conventions in the country and lasts for ten days.

When I ran for election to be a deputy from the Diocese of Atlanta in November 2002, I wasn't thinking about resolutions. I was thinking about wonderful worship, incredible preaching, and famous people—a kind of ecclesial Woodstock. I had wanted to go to General Convention ever since childhood. I had seen a certificate in my grandmother's house congratulating Martha S. Flud, my great aunt, for contributing to the Children's Lenten Offering for the 1889 General Convention in New York City. I imagined it to be like Disneyland. As a teenager I thought of it like the United Nations. In my adult years, I thought of it as a kind of festival. I'd get to see all the people I had read and heard about: Frank Griswold, the head of the church; Barbara Harris, the first woman to be ordained a bishop; Verna Dozier, a champion for the ministry of the laity.

Then history intruded on my ten-day church festival. In June of 2003, the Episcopal Diocese of New Hampshire elected the Rev. Gene Robinson as their next bishop. Because of a quirk of the By-Laws, he had to be confirmed by a majority of the bishops and a majority of the laity and clergy deputies attending the General Convention, or he couldn't be a bishop. He was not the only bishop-elect to be voted on here; there were six others. But he was the only openly gay bishop elect—anywhere, anytime.

Once Gene Robinson hit the news, people were calling and emailing me to ask about my position. I received propaganda in the mail from organizations with names that began with "Episcopalians"—Episcopalians for Biblical Orthodoxy, Episcopalians for Life, and more.

The protestor, the signs, and my mail were clues that this was not going to be easy or short-lived. It was going to be history.

It was Wednesday, July 30, the first of the ten days. Every day of convention had two parts, worship and business. The day started with the Holy Eucharist followed by legislative sessions until the evening. I walked into the hall for the Eucharist, a huge space with small circular tables surrounding a raised dais. A bronze cross was suspended over the altar. Behind the stage was a screen with rotating images of people of all races and ages and a banner that read "Engage God's Mission: The 74th General Convention." Assigned to table 102, I began hunting. All conversation was drowned out by the choir singing from the back of the room, "I Come with Joy to Greet the Lord."

There were seven other people at table 102. I sat next to a middle-aged woman from a Florida diocese. She had dirt-brown hair that flipped up at her shoulders and reminded me of the Donna Reed of my childhood. She wore a dark-blue dress and looked like a flight attendant. Next to her was a woman from Upper South Carolina—thin and tall with sharp features and close-cropped blonde hair. If I were using John King's CNN election map, these definitely represented bright red states. Also, there was a priest from the American Churches in Europe. Next to him was a white-haired man wearing a blue seersucker suit with a red bow tie, who turned out to be a bishop from one of the larger dioceses.

The procession came in—red and blue robes, incense, banners, a handful of bishops. *This is what I came for.* We prayed, heard the scriptures read, sang hymns.

The Presiding Bishop, Frank Griswold, came to the pulpit for the sermon. He wore the traditional glossy white robes and a large gold cross centered on his chest. He spoke with a patrician Philadelphia accent. The longer he talked, the more my mind wandered. I was more interested in the people around me. It was alphabet soup. A man one table over wore a tailored khaki suit. Beside him was a teenage boy in shorts and a green T-shirt with "Engage" on the front. A few tables over was a woman in a green wraparound skirt and a pink sweater. She had a long blonde ponytail to her waist. Beside her was a woman in a severe black pantsuit that made her look as if she belonged in the FBI. The only norm was The Book of Common Prayer we held in our hands.

Finally, the Presiding Bishop's cadence changed. "This is the prayer of a Russian bishop in the nineteenth century."

How esoteric could he get? But then the prayer made me ashamed of that thought.

"Lord, grant me grace to greet the coming day in peace. Help me in all things to rely on your holy will."

We all said, "Amen" hoping that would make it so.

After the sermon, we were to have table discussions for thirty minutes. The Florida woman spoke first. "If we approve Gene Robinson, my diocese will leave the church. I have been an Episcopalian all my life. I feel like my church is being hijacked."

Long silence. Upper South Carolina spoke, "Me too. I don't know what the rush is. Why can't we just think about this for another three years? Why now?"

The bishop said in a professorial tone, "It's not about sexuality. It's about the right of a diocese to choose its own bishop. I don't agree with it, but I can't see why we should stop it."

I found myself torn between head and heart—as always.

I had long ago resolved any theological or scriptural reservations about full inclusion of gays and lesbians in the church. The Bible wasn't the last word; it was the living word. We are called to bring the sacred word into conversation with the contemporary world. Otherwise, we'd believe all kinds of odd notions—such as males being the only real factor in reproductivity, or polygamy for that matter. There are seven passages of scripture against homosexuality, and I had worked through all of them to ensure that there was no biblical prohibition.

I would vote for Gene Robinson. Yes, we as the church had done all this backward. We were acting before we fully articulated our theology, but that's the way Episcopalians do most things. The rightness of including gays and lesbians in all orders of the church outweighed the mess.

My problems weren't in my head. They were in my heart. As the poet Anne Sexton wrote about St. Teresa: "I have no defense against affection. I could be bribed with a sardine."[1] Me too. I had no defense against pain either. I absorbed it. I carried it. I ate it and hoped my body would somehow transmute it. Others' hurt became my responsibility, and it didn't matter how many books on codependency I read, my skin didn't get any thicker. In my head I knew that change, by definition, is disruptive and tumultuous. Intellectually I understood that all movements require shaking the foundations. But my heart could not steel itself from opening up to the suffering that comes with that shaking.

On my first Sunday at my church in Athens, Georgia, a young woman stood in the adult forum and said, "I am a lesbian. I have been with my partner for five years. Is there a place in this church for me?"

---

1. Sexton, "Saints Come Marching In," 470.

I said, "Of course. There's a place for everyone. I hope you and your partner come so we can learn from each other what it means to be church."

I felt so proud of myself for saying the right answer. But my heart fell when a maintenance man for the university came to my office Monday afternoon in his green jumpsuit and said, "I think I have to quit the church if you're inviting homosexuals."

"Jim, a place for everyone means you too." I grabbed his arm. "We need your voice here." But what I thought was, *Don't let me be the one who divides this church my first week.* I lost sleep for a week wondering if Jim would be in church next Sunday.

For me, Gene Robinson was not a theological problem but a spiritual problem. It was about letting go. Could I rely on God's holy will? Could I let God be God and be content to tend to my small corner of the world? Did I believe God was working God's purpose out even when it made people's lives a mess?

I said to the others at the table: "We are in a crazy place because we haven't done our homework. We don't have a liturgy to bless relationships. We haven't warned the rest of the Anglican world. We haven't even voted to say gays and lesbians can be bishops. But here we are. We are going to approve a person and do our theology later. The truth is we've always been upside down."

I looked at the Florida woman. "I know the ground underneath our feet is going to shake."

"God have mercy on us," she said.

\* \* \*

"Hey Porter, what are you doing here?"

Finally, I saw a familiar face. I was wading through the 1000 other people jammed into a cavernous windowless convention hall. Deputies were streaming in from worship. Already people had started using their name badges to advertise their causes with metal pins. I saw many rainbows, the symbol of Integrity, the primary organization supporting gay and lesbian issues. The meeting had not started, so people filled the aisles between the long rows of tables. I was looking for Atlanta's table marked H-2, but I couldn't see any of the signs.

"Bam, don't you remember me?" She addressed me by my childhood name that I mostly escaped at forty.

"Oh, hey. I'm sorry. I've never seen anything like this."

She and I had attended seminary together. She had a church in New Orleans and, like me, was a deputy. She looked like one of the fairy godmothers in the Disney "Cinderella"—short, plump, and fun. She wore her black clergy shirt with a white collar and bright silver cross. A large square name badge told me she was Susan from Louisiana.

"You know I am going to take a beating voting for Gene Robinson," she said.

"I think we are all going to take a beating."

Finally, I saw the Diocese of Atlanta table, sandwiched between Navajo land and Michigan. We were about three rows from the main dais on the right edge of the hall.

As I walked through the rows of rectangular tables, I kept seeing men and women with three-inch buttons that said, "Ask me about Gene." So, I asked a tall man dressed in a clergy shirt and blue jeans. "Where is he?"

"Table F-7. Back left corner."

I knew it was him because he wore a big blue button that said, "I'm Gene." Gene Robinson turned out to be short and slim with delicate small hands. Balding, he wore rimless glasses. What I felt first was his energy. He was laughing and talking and nodding all at once to the person next to him. I reached over to shake his hand and noticed a large bulky man move between me and the Reverend Robinson.

"It's okay," the bishop elect said, turning to the protector. "Once we are in this room, you can relax."

"You have a bodyguard? Sorry. I'm Porter Taylor. From Atlanta. I just wanted to meet you."

"Great to see you Porter," he said with a laugh. "Yes, well, interesting times."

Then the gavel banged. "Good luck Reverend Robinson."

"Gene. Call me Gene, and thanks."

The session left me unengaged. We talked about the budget, argued about whether to defund the National Defense Department, said "thank you" to everyone who lived in Minneapolis, and declared we were against trafficking of women, girls, and boys. We voted by pressing a remote control that was more complicated than the one I had at home from Charter Communications. My mind wasn't there. I kept thinking about the bodyguard. It felt like Thomas à Becket. *Have we as a church not learned anything? Is this really the institution I want to represent?* It was one thing for me and the woman from Central Florida to worry about the church dividing, but bodyguards?

When I told my Atlanta seatmate about it, she said, "Did you look at his chest?"

"His chest? You mean to see his cross or nametag?"

"He's wearing a bulletproof vest."

"I thought we were the church."

"Porter, welcome behind the curtain. This is the church in all its glory and disgrace."

\* \* \*

On the evening of Day Three, Friday, August 1, a hearing was held concerning the question of consenting to a gay bishop. The Episcopal Church is orderly. Each speaker had two minutes and the speakers alternated between pro and con. They had to sign up hours before the event. There were enough speakers to speak until breakfast but thank God, only two hours were allotted.

The first speaker was a bishop representing the very conservative wing. Short, dark suit two sizes too big, fuzzy black hair, and long wild eyelashes that stuck out like fins from his face. He spoke in a soft sort of Garrison Keillor voice, but that belied the content. "This is heresy. It's against the Bible; it's against God's design; it's immoral. I warn you," he said. "This is the end of the church."

Then a priest from Atlanta spoke for the other side. His white linen suit reminded me of Atticus Finch in *To Kill a Mockingbird*. "Scripture interprets scripture. That's what Jesus did. 'You have heard it said, but I say to you.' Consecrating Gene Robinson isn't heresy. It's the Good News. In Christ there is no male or female and no straight or gay."

And so it went. The low point of the evening occurred when a priest from Springfield, Illinois, described in detail anal sex and the diseases that could be caught during male-to-male sex. When he finished, there was a dead silence. Enough.

My hotel room in the Hilton, a few blocks from the Convention Center, was small. A bed, a chair, a table, a TV, and a bath. The view from my window was nothing more than other hotels or office buildings. Within three days, I had developed a sharp pain down my right arm. I had tried putting a tennis ball between my shoulder blade and the wall, as a do-it-yourself massage, but it didn't help. That morning I had gone down to the whirlpool, but the relief didn't last.

The pain took away my sleep. Though I fell asleep quickly, I woke around two or three o'clock with a stinging sensation that followed the nerve down my arm. I tried hot showers. I tried my tennis ball against the wall. I tried listening to the BBC. I tried reading Donna Leon's mysteries. Early one morning I tried walking in the stillness of Minneapolis streets, but nothing worked.

The morning of the fourth day I called my doctor in Athens, Georgia, and asked for some painkillers. After I described the symptoms to his nurse, she said, "Find a Walgreens and we'll call in an order." Fortunately, there was one across the street. I was confident I would sleep that night. But it wasn't to be. The Deputies were to vote on Gene Robinson on Sunday, Day Five.

\* \* \*

The preacher Sunday morning was a bishop from Africa. I was afraid he would condemn The Episcopal Church because I knew he was very conservative, but he was filled with proper Anglican restraint. At the end of his sermon, he said, "Our church family takes The Episcopal Church very seriously. When America sneezes, the rest of the world catches a cold. America, don't sneeze too much."

Because we didn't gather at our tables this day for discussion, I had no idea what my tablemate from Florida was going through.

We assembled in the Convention Hall at 2:30. At 2:50 we began debating whether to approve Gene Robinson as the next bishop of New Hampshire. Each speaker was given two minutes. They stood on platforms scattered amid the deputies' tables. When each person's time was up, a light above their head began to blink. The line to speak snaked to the back of the Deputies' section. This session went on for thirty minutes.

I wore my gray suit and black clergy shirt and collar with my seminary silver cross hanging above my heart. I held my small hand-size Book of Common Prayer with both hands. I was only half listening to the speakers. Instead, I repeated over and over in my head, "Show us the way."

I could hear a priest crying as she asked the hall from one of the platforms, "What will I tell my children after this about what is moral and what isn't? Do we as a church not stand for anything?"

I could hear an officer from Integrity, the organization advocating for LGBTQ rights in The Episcopal Church, proclaim, "We have journeyed a long way and we are almost on the mountaintop. The path of history is long but bends toward justice."

I could hear a layperson from the Midwest say, "My grandmother always told me fear is the absence of faith. You may be afraid of schism. Do not be afraid."

"Show us the way."

"This is what change looks like," I told myself. "I am here to do what I think is right and to let go of the results. It's God's church and I am one vote." But that was my head talking. My heart felt this church ripping apart. It was like anticipating a tsunami, knowing high ground is too far away.

The debate was extended another fifteen minutes. Then the President of the Deputies called on the Chaplain. "Come Holy Spirit," he prayed.

Before the vote, we had ten minutes of silence. Nine hundred people completely still. In the back of the hall the reporters were all roped off. CNN, ABC, and others were all there. Somehow they were still as well.

In that silence I prayed, "Help me remember this silent moment. Let me remember the sense of Christ holding us all in his arms when the splintering begins."

Then we voted "by orders," which means the clergy voted separate from the laypeople but both "orders" had to affirm. Each of us was handed a ballot on which to check YES or NO and then sign our name beside our vote. There was a deep pause in the hall, a moment before our world might be changed forever.

The vote was overwhelming. Out of the 109 dioceses, the Clergy voted in favor 65 to 31 and the Laity voted in favor 63 to 32. To be counted, three of the four deputies had to agree. Otherwise, if it was a two-to-two vote, the ballot was considered "divided" and didn't count.

That silent peace was broken by the movement that fear or anger or despair can bring. Deputies from the Dioceses of South Carolina, Pittsburgh, Springfield, and Fort Worth stood up and walked out of the hall in a silent procession. Those from Fort Worth were reported to have poured salt on the floor to ward off evil as they departed.

Loud noise came from the rear of the room as the reporters blurted their questions. "What will happen to the church now?" "Will you be kicked out of the Anglican Communion?" "Some of the bishops say you are heretics. What do you say to that?"

The Chaplain came to the microphone and restored order. "Come Holy Spirit," he prayed. "Where there is sorrow, assist us to help; where there is confusion, assist us to find clarity." The gavel banged.

Chaos. Cheers. Pairs wept as they held one another. A large crowd formed around the New Hampshire table. People were singing and laughing and crying and shouting and staring into space. Amid the swirl some deputies were simply sitting—caught in the turn of history.

The cacophony of the press and the bright lights of the television cameras reminded me that my parishioners were hearing this news, and I had no clear idea of what they were thinking. I left the hall to write an email to my parish, explaining my vote.

My email ended with, "There are cries of schism and moral chaos. I do not believe them. The church will change as she has always changed, but the election of Gene Robinson is a tremor not an earthquake. God will work God's purpose out in God's good time and in God's good way. Our task is to not be afraid, to listen to what God is calling us to do, and then have the grace and the courage to respond."

I wrote these words to convince myself.

The bishops were to vote on Monday.

\* \* \*

The bishops did not vote on Monday. One of the very conservative Episcopal organizations, The American Anglican Council, presented two charges to the Presiding Bishop to discredit Gene Robinson. One claimed that a website "associated" with the Rev. Robinson had a link to a pornographic site. The second was a claim by a man stating that Gene had touched him in an inappropriate way during two encounters at church meetings far in the past.

I tried to stay on the high road, but I kept thinking that Satan is the Prince of Lies. Bodyguards, bullet-proof vests, and now flimsy outrageous accusations at the last minute. The Presiding Bishop appointed the Bishop of Western Massachusetts to investigate and report back to the bishops.

Monday went on as if nothing had happened. I noticed empty tables here and there. The business chugged along.

Monday afternoon I asked an alternate deputy to take my place on the Convention floor and walked to the Minneapolis Museum of Art. I gazed at Van Gogh's *Olive Trees*. Twisted trunks and branches framed a blue mountain and bright yellow sun. The ground under the trees was swirling. The life force seemed so benign on canvas.

\* \* \*

At the Eucharist on Tuesday, August 5, the woman from Florida sat wringing her hands. Her face was red and puffy. Her hair no longer flipped up but was tied in a knot. She looked at the table as she spoke. "My bishop says if Gene Robinson is approved, our whole diocese is leaving the church. Half of our deputation has already left the Convention Center. I keep getting emails and phone calls from people asking me to do something, but what can I do?"

I said, "You are one person. You can't be responsible for all this. Let's see what happens this afternoon." I was talking to myself. My arm pain had only gotten worse. I walked to the Convention Center looking as though my collarbone was broken. I hadn't slept the night before.

The charges against Gene Robinson were dismissed in the morning business session. The bishops were to vote late in the afternoon. Their meeting was closed to the public for an hour before they voted. Later I learned that they prayed and anointed one another as they lay hands on one another's heads. When the doors opened and the public came in, the room was quickly mobbed. I watched from one of the television monitors in the hallway away from the crowd.

The bishops sat at round tables. The roll was called alphabetically, and each said his or her vote.

Alabama—No

Albany—No

Alaska—Yes

Atlanta—Yes

Passing required fifty-five votes—sixty-two bishops voted Yes. The Episcopal Church took a step beyond what was safe into a land of discord which was also that of faithfulness. I did not remain for the aftermath of the vote. Later I heard that a dozen bishops immediately read a statement rejecting the action. I took a walk around the streets of Minneapolis.

I kept thinking of the William Butler Yeats quote: "All changed, changed utterly: A terrible beauty is born."[2] A terrible beauty was born on that day in our church. It was painful and wonderful all at once.

* * *

That night I fell asleep and slept through the night. For a moment I felt the peace the world can't give or take away.

Early in the morning I had a dream that my son, Arthur, then nineteen, was driving in Athens late at night. It was raining. His white Volvo 240, the car his mother and I had bought to keep him safe, started fishing to the left. He kept turning the wheel back, but he could not stop the skid. The car slid off the road. The front fender hit a tree, and Arthur's head hit the windshield. The front door was jarred open, and his body flopped sideways halfway out of the car. Blood poured down his face and hair into the wet earth. He lay unmoving with his arms outstretched as if in surrender.

---

2. Yeats, "Easter 1916," 177.

I woke screaming "Arthur." I wiped my face. Tears streamed down my cheeks.

The red numerals of the hotel clock said 3:00 a.m. I was petrified. My son was dead. I called Jo. The phone rang and rang.

Finally, a groggy, "Hello."

"Is Arthur home? Is he alright?"

"Bam? What is going on? It's three in the morning."

"Is he alright?"

"Of course, he's alright. What is wrong with you?"

"How do you know? Go into his bedroom and see. Wake him up."

A long pause. "Bam? Are you okay?"

"I know how it sounds, but please do it. Please."

For a few minutes I listened to my heart pound in my chest. I stared at the hotel wall. I was holding my chest with the arm that throbbed. "Please," I prayed. "Please."

"He's fine. He's wondering if his father has gone off the deep end, but he's fine."

"It's so confusing up here. I'll call you in the morning. Just a bad dream."

\* \* \*

As I neared the Convention Center, no one greeted me or accosted me or cared about me. The protesters and CNN had left. The sign said that The Episcopal Church still welcomed me, but everyone else had moved on.

Many seats were empty in the worship hall. Table 102 was half empty. The priest from Europe and the bishop from Virginia were there. To my surprise, the Florida woman was there.

"I'm so glad you are here," I said, sitting beside her.

"I almost didn't come, but it's still my church too."

"I am guessing you feel our church has died, and maybe it has. But last night I thought my son had died, and I had a brief sense of your loss."

I told her about my dream.

She said, "We are supposed to believe in resurrection, but I can't see it. All I see is loss and pain. You woke up and it's all okay, but what about me?"

"I don't know," I said. "But let's believe in resurrection anyway. Let's pray for life on the other side of all our losses."

She didn't reply. She looked down at the table.

"I hope we see each other at the next Convention in 2006," I said.

She looked up. Her voice was soft as if it came from a place far from this hall. "Porter, that's too much to hope for. Let's hope there's still an Episcopal Church in 2006."

In his sermon, the Presiding Bishop quoted the Sufi poet Rumi: "Out beyond ideas of wrongdoing and rightdoing there is a field. I'll meet you there."[3]

I prayed for that field, and I prayed God would bring us all there.

---

3. Rumi, "Out Beyond Ideas of Wrongdoing and Rightdoing," 36.

# 6

# The Election

Our job is to hold a post in the resonant field. Keep your attention in yourself.
Keep within, don't let your attention be scrambled. Don't fall asleep. Look for
opportunities to be present and give presence.

—Cynthia Bourgeault, *Centering Prayer and Inner
Awakening*

"I don't know what to do with myself."

Jo didn't respond. She kept leaning over to weed her flower garden. She
looked like a swan with its head thrust in the water and her backside held
up to the air. Here the water was purple irises. I could see the handles of her
shears sticking out of her back pocket like a 1960s peace sign. Our garden
ran along the front walkway. Jo had brought these irises from our house in
Nashville eight years before. They reminded her of our life before the church
took it over.

May 1, 2004 was a perfect spring morning in Athens, Georgia. The
smothering summer heat was still in Florida and wouldn't come to Georgia
until July. At nine o'clock on a Saturday morning, the neighborhood had yet
to stir. This far into the suburbs, especially on our dead-end street, there
were no festivals of spring, no maypoles, and certainly no celebrations of
turning over regimes by Marxist workers. The day was still and settled.

Jo stayed in the irises.

"I just don't know what to do with myself," I said louder with an edge.

Her torso lifted out of the flower bed, but she kept her feet planted, and twisted around to see me. Her face was flush from bending over, and she wiped the hair from her face with her forearms because her gloved hands were covered with mulch and Georgia clay.

"There's nothing you can do about the election. Come work with me in the garden. Weeding will be better for you than worrying about being a bishop."

For a short while, I moved into the iris bed and kicked at the weeds as an alternative to thinking about possible futures. I could not muster any enthusiasm for weeding, but I knew I didn't want to pace the dining room floors waiting for the voting. There was no place to go. I stood beside Jo as if I were one of the valets in some Masterpiece Theatre program.

* * *

In 2004 I was a priest in charge of a small parish in Athens, Georgia—St. Gregory the Great Episcopal Church, or as I used to say, St. Gregory, the great Episcopal church. I had been their rector for eight years and loved it most of that time. However, I had gone on a three-month sabbatical in 2002. After a month in Italy and two weeks in a monastery, I never quite settled back in. I had become ambivalent about the sameness.

Part of me felt as if I were repeating myself. I feared becoming a juke-box. It's Christmas so I'll punch in B-15—wreath, pageant, sweet sermon about the baby, candles, "Silent Night" and done. I didn't want to spend the last ten years of my ordained ministry going through the motions. On the other hand, the weekly routine was comfortable and predictable. Tuesday was staff meeting. Wednesday I visited hospitals. Thursday I wrote my sermon. Friday I did everything else. Saturday I did this and that before Sunday church, and Monday I collapsed. Weeks into months into eight years. What had happened to my life? Here Jo and I were, fifty-three years old with a son in college and a daughter in high school. We had been married for thirty-one years. We had professional jobs. Both our walls were filled with diplomas, and we both had initials behind our names. But I felt that we were coasting or that our lives had somehow become vanilla.

Perhaps that feeling led to my response to the phone call in August of 2003. Out of the blue, I received a call from Danny, the only high school friend with whom I still had contact.

"Bam, how'd you like to be Bishop of Western North Carolina?"

"Why would anyone want me to do that?"

"I think you'd be great. Can I put your name in?"

Instead of saying, "Let me think about it," I simply said, "Yes." I didn't know why. I never thought about bishops. The bishop in Atlanta came to visit St. Gregory once every other year and it was like having your parents visit you in college. We cleaned everything up and put on our best show so that our daddy would give us a gold star. As his car went out the driveway, we breathed a huge sigh, went back to our customary disorder, and forgot about him until the next time.

When my friend asked me, I didn't think of the Atlanta bishop, however; I thought of Bishop Henry, the bishop of my childhood in Western North Carolina. A church version of Teddy Roosevelt. Short, but with a thunderous voice and a handshake that few people forgot. A man without "maybe" in his vocabulary. He planted churches. He told young men to go to seminary. He built an Episcopal retirement center, and he started a school for boys. Bishop Henry was what we now call one of the "princes of the church." He asked people's opinion about as often as Moses did in the forty years of wandering in the desert. People still tell stories of him grabbing their arm in his firm grip and not letting go until he asked a favor.

He confirmed me when I was twelve, in 1962. Sally, my twin sister, got a new dress and I got a new blue blazer with a gray handkerchief sewn into the front pocket. I put on my Bass Weejuns and added an extra dollop of Vitalis to my hair, totally forgetting that the bishop would have to put his hands on that goo. There were fourteen of us to be confirmed. We sat on the front of row of Trinity Church, Asheville, looking like substitutes in a basketball game praying the coach wouldn't put us in. The church was as big as an air hanger. The bishop sat in a chair between the choir stalls and looked like Henry VIII with his bright red and crisp white vestments. He leaned on his shepherd's crook and looked out at the congregation as if to say, "This is my church."

I completely lost my place in the service. Acolytes and priests and lay readers moved around, but I had no idea why. I was hoping the bishop had forgotten about us. None of my friends knew my given name. Somehow "Granville Porter" had been shortened to "Bam" when my sister and I were speaking our two-year-old-twin language. Everything was going to come out today. The bishop would see what a fraud I was as a prepared Christian, much less Episcopalian, and the congregation would witness how clumsy a twelve-year-old could be. I knew I'd hear "Granny" jokes for the duration of junior high.

At some point, the usher waved us to stand before the bishop. One by one we went up the carpeted steps and knelt on a purple cushion before the bishop. I remember he had lacy cuffs on his vestments and a huge purple ring on his right hand. When I looked up at him, I felt that he could see through me. Then he gripped my head, and I closed my eyes. He squeezed my head harder and harder. When I heard his baritone voice intone "Defend O Lord your servant Granville with your heavenly grace," I thought it was the voice of God making me into a Christian soldier.

I knew that this meant I could take communion, but I didn't know what else it meant. Maybe I was connected to him, and somehow I could count on him. He was a kind of Aslan figure for me. I liked being a big deal at coffee hour after the service although I thought a red Book of Common Prayer was a pretty lame gift. At twelve I thought this was all bishops did— go from church to church laying hands on adolescents' heads.

It's too bad I didn't remember more about the first bishop's family the day my friend called about the nomination. His children went to school with me. The daughter was a year younger and the son two years older. Occasionally, I'd hang out at their house, and I'd see them at school, football games, and church youth group. However, I never saw their father. He didn't come to any school events, and I never saw him around the house on Saturdays. That should have been a clue as to what a bishop's life was like.

*  *  *

In March of 2004, I received a call from the priest who was head of the Bishop's Search Committee. "Porter, you are one of four priests who will be on the ballot for the election on May 1."

I immediately went to the family computer to look up the other three. One candidate was the hometown boy. He had been in the diocese his entire ordained career. Smart—doctorate degree from Yale. Big marathon runner. The second candidate looked like someone who would testify before a Senate committee—smart, dapper, smooth, assistant to the bishop in another diocese. He'd been a priest for many years and done everything. And, his long list of outside interests included raku pottery, organ music, Chinese poetry. He looked like one of those guys on insurance commercials. "Call me if you have a problem, because I can fix anything." I'd vote for him.

The third nominee seemed to be the man of the people. Showing a mustache, he appeared to be the kind of person who could shoot the breeze for hours. He'd been a chaplain in the Navy and he'd been in charge of a large church in Florida.

And then there was me. I wondered who in the world had come up with the content in my bio. It made me sound like a nerd who spent his life in libraries and monasteries. "He served as an associate professor at Belmont College in Nashville, Tennessee, as a Fulbright Lecturer at the University of Oporto, Portugal," and so on. "Taylor is fifty-three and has continuing education in spiritual life." What did that mean? Is there someone who isn't continuing their education in spiritual life? My dad used to say, "Those who can do; those who can't teach." This sounded as if I had a PhD in "can't." I knew I had no prayer. I wouldn't even vote for me. Who would want what Spiro Agnew called "an effete snob" as their bishop? The only information that might win me votes was the part about growing up in Asheville and going to Trinity Church.

* * *

There are times when I think it would have been easier to buy a convertible or go to Haiti as an aid worker than become a bishop. In 2004 I was afraid my life was going to run out without my making a visible mark. I had published a book of sermons. I had baptized countless new Christians and buried the dead and anointed the sick and consoled the dispirited and married all ages of couples. I had said my prayers and tried to be faithful. But I could not measure any accomplishment.

I remember as a six-year-old when my dad took me to his sweater company in Weaverville, North Carolina, one Saturday morning. Only he and I were there. I got to sit at his secretary's desk and play with her adding machine and I sang songs into her dictating machine and ran up and down the aisles between the green-painted knitting machines.

On the way home I said, "Dad, I know how to be a daddy and how to be a husband, but how do you be a businessman?"

"Don't worry," he said. "You'll figure it out."

I am not sure I had, and that uncertainty in part pushed me to try this new thing. I thought bishops made things happen. I thought they had power and influence. I thought, this is what you are supposed to do. It is the next step for a successful career.

At the office of the Diocese of Atlanta, the portraits of past bishops hang on the corridor walls, resembling Civil War generals—stoic, decisive, sure.

Whatever I thought about bishops, I didn't think enough.

* * *

Even after the election, even after years of being a bishop in the church, I was discerning my vocation. I thought I was elected to make a mark, to lead the church into going deeper in her faith, and witness to the world.

In June 2008 I went on a retreat at the monastery in Moncks Corner, South Carolina, to look at my vocation. I took the brown Bible I received at my bishop's ordination and my palm-sized Book of Common Prayer with its black spine now cracked from my daily use.

I sat in the refectory—a long rectangular room—most of the daytime, looking out the window at the live oaks and the Spanish moss stirred by the wind. The room has rose-colored tiles and crisp white walls. The tables were yellow pine and glowed from the South Carolina sun.

I drank herbal tea and ate peanut butter crackers and read the epistles. I wanted to see how those early Christians were able to push forward and start a movement.

The third day, I met with the monk who was the guest master. He was in his late sixties, slightly bent over. His hair was white and wispy, circling his bald spot. He spent his days working the gardens and seemed disappointed that I did not help him with his latest project—building a labyrinth made from wildflowers. In the monk's sitting room, we sat in two straight chairs facing one another. Over his head was a painting of Mary holding her crucified son.

"What is troubling you? You seem lost," he said.

"I've lost the thread. I can't remember why I am doing this. And sometimes I don't think I do it very well. Plus, I have no life anymore. I'm not Porter. I'm just the bishop." I confessed this in my quietest voice because even to say it aloud in this safe place was still somehow shameful.

His voice was soft, and he had a slight lisp. "Well. This is what Meister Eckhart says, 'Look for God where you lost him.'" He smiled and said, "Of course, he was a heretic."

Then he told me to reread my ordination vows and to pray on them. "Go back to the beginning."

That afternoon I was back in the refectory—herbal tea, crackers, Book of Common Prayer. I read the vows, but I had almost no memory of saying them. I opened my prayer book, moving my lips as I read them. In the final prayer, I saw this line as if for the first time: *May [the new bishop] present before [God] the acceptable offering of a pure, and gentle, and holy life.*[1]

Was that enough? Would pure or gentle or holy get anything done? Didn't people like Mayor Daley make cities work? Wasn't my problem that I was too ethereal? Still continuing my education in the spiritual life? Or was it that I had no center and had become just an ornate suit?

I stopped the brother in the middle of the emerging labyrinth the next day. He wore his white habit with the black scapular (the cloth that hangs in

---

1. *The Book of Common Prayer*, 517.

the front and back). His hat looked almost like a sombrero, its white brim shadowing his entire face. His face was flush from the work and the heat and his happiness at his creation.

"Why seek to be holy if your job is to get things done?"

He leaned on his rake. "Porter. You are asking the wrong question," he said. "It's about your salvation. It's all about your salvation. Who do you think is responsible for anything happening anyway? Is God a player or not?"

"Well," I said, "it doesn't feel like it. The truth is, I am so isolated. I feel stuck in a bubble. I have no church home, anymore. I come and do the magic and then leave but I am not part of any community. And I don't feel as if I have done enough. I think my epitaph will be 'He kept up with his email.'"

He looked at me for several moments. "Do you know anything about labyrinths?"

"Sort of."

"Well," he said, and took his hat off as he wiped his brow. "Here's the key. You can't get lost. Once you start, all you have to do is walk and you are guaranteed to get to the center."

But when I looked at his labyrinth, only half the paths were made. The rest was an empty field.

* * *

The last Saturday of March 2004, the Diocese of WNC held their "walk-about" which all the clergy call "the dog and pony show." The candidates travel in a bus to locations in the diocese so that Episcopalians can meet them and ask them trick questions. WNC actually was more benevolent than most places because they only scheduled two sessions on a Saturday: one in Hickory and one in Waynesville.

The eight of us—nominees and wives—plus the twelve members of the nominating committee boarded a bus in Asheville early Saturday morning to go to Waynesville. One of the candidates walked up and down the aisle of the bus burning off his anxiety by talking.

I whispered to Jo, "If that guy starts to talk to me, I am going to lose it."

"Just breathe," she said.

As we drove along I-40, it wasn't that I wanted to win; I didn't want to look like a fool. I hadn't been ordained that long. I'd never done anything on a national level except vote for Gene Robinson in 2003 which could be seen as both good and bad news. I kept going through my rolodex of hot-button issues. Younger Vocations? Talk about the University of Georgia and campus ministry. Same Sex Blessings? Obfuscate with mumbo jumbo about General Convention and the process. Cursillo? Pretend you like the music.

I felt Jo clamp her hand on my knee and I realized I was bouncing both knees up and down. "Be still," she said. "What do you need to get centered?"

"Swap seats with me."

I sat next to the window and looked out at the mountains passing by. I didn't think about the questions for the day or the vote to come in five weeks or anything. I stared at the blue-green bell curves against the sky. I remembered going to Canton in the eighth grade, in the red David Millard bus, to play the Pisgah Bears. I was certain that the mountain boys would cream us, but it was the other way around. Once the game started, the D.M. Terriers ran up and down the field.

We had eight sessions, four in each place. The day was fine until the last room. We were in a classroom in Church of the Ascension, Hickory. It felt as if I were back teaching high school English. It was about 4:30 and we had been at this since 9:00 a.m.

A short woman in a green dress stood and asked, "What about the diocese's debt? Did you know we owe the bank five-and-a-half million dollars? What's your plan for that?"

I had no clue. The diocese had sold their old conference center and bought a new one. What was supposed to be a wash ended up in a sea of red.

"Well," I began. "The question is not about the debt. It's about the church's mission. If we get clear about how to use the conference center for God's work, I'm sure the money will follow. Folks don't usually give for debt, but they do when something's going on."

She didn't nod and she didn't smile. Instead, she widened her eyes as if to say, "Are you for real?"

Then a man in the back stood and asked about same sex something. He wore a dark suit and suspender pants—which meant you couldn't have seen his belt if he had worn one. I asked him to repeat his question. "What about blessings and marriage? What will you do to preserve the sanctity of marriage?"

I was tired. My head hurt. I had been standing and answering questions for two hours without a break and I had to pee. Plus, about halfway through the day, I realized I was selling myself, which only made the intensity greater. I wasn't sure why I wanted this so badly, but I did.

The night before, Jo and I had stayed in an antiseptic bedroom at the Episcopal retirement center. I couldn't sleep and ended up reading my mystery novel in a chair in the hall for a few hours. If only I could be Harry

Bosch tomorrow—the detective created by Michael Connelly. But Harry Bosch was too smart to run for bishop.

And yet, for some time I sat in the chair not seeing the words. The words that came to me were, "Please God. Please give this to me."

I looked at the clock in the Hickory classroom. I knew the questions were almost over. I was so tired I didn't care anymore. The green-dress woman had helped me realize how futile it was to please all these people.

"Sir, I think you are talking about apples and oranges. If we want to support the sanctity of marriage, we need fewer divorces. That means we ought to work on minimum wage or shorten the work week or ensure that families have daycare. This isn't so much a moral problem as an economic one."

Dead silence. The man started to stand back up, but the moderator stood and held up both hands.

"Thank you, Father Taylor. Maybe one more question."

A priest in his forties stood. He wore a black clerical shirt, was bald, and had on clear glasses. He looked like a California transplant. "Why do you want to be our bishop?"

I looked at him. I looked over his head to the blank wall and then down at my feet. For a moment I couldn't think of an answer I could say.

"Well. I love the church. And I think we are in turbulent times. And I'd like to help get us to a better place."

The priest's eyebrows were raised as if to say, "That's it?" I nodded my head. That was it.

On the bus ride back to Asheville, everyone was subdued. About half-way there, one of the candidates stood and asked in his deep baritone, "Hey, how about we all go to dinner together?"

I said, "I don't think so."

\* \* \*

The first ballot was scheduled for ten o'clock a.m. at Trinity Church, Asheville. In the Episcopal Church in Western North Carolina every parish elects two lay people to vote, and every priest and deacon get a vote. To be elected requires a majority of lay votes and of clergy—much like the United States House of Representatives and the Senate. My experience told me that when there is a split, the clergy usually move to vote with the laity, but my experience was also limited to voting in two elections in other dioceses.

What bothered me was that the results would be public. The Diocese of WNC was to post them on their website as soon they were tabulated. I had been in rector searches before, but when they chose someone else, at least your rejection was private. I didn't need to win, but I didn't want goose eggs either.

At ten o'clock in the morning I went into our son's room and turned on the family computer. There was nothing posted yet. I went back to the garden. Jo had moved on to starting a new bed for tomatoes. "Why don't you dig up some dirt?" she said. But I couldn't. I was wearing blue jeans and a "How Bout Them Dogs" T-shirt. I kept pushing my hands deep into my back pockets as if somehow that would root me into the earth and help me be still.

Marie, our daughter, yelled from the front door. "Dad, the first ballot's in." I received forty-one clergy and forty-six lay votes. The candidate from the diocese had fifty-one clergy and forty-four lay. The requirement for election was sixty-five clergy and seventy-three lay votes.

I looked at the numbers. My prideful self was relieved not to have come in last. Coming in second would be okay. I wouldn't embarrass myself, and our lives wouldn't get turned inside out. The tension in the back of my neck eased some and I took a deep breath.

"Jo, we're in the running, but it's probably going to be the hometown boy."

"Well, I'd hate to think I was planting these tomatoes for nothing."

"Why don't I help you?"

She gave me a look that said, "Are you kidding me?" I quietly picked up a shovel and dug in the dirt.

* * *

When the final numbers came in about one thirty, the phone started ringing and didn't stop until the batteries died. The candidate from within the diocese had fifty-four clergy votes and fifty lay. I received sixty-seven clergy votes and eighty-six lay. Two more than needed from the clergy and thirteen over the required votes from the laity. I looked at the screen and went into the garden. Jo looked across the yard, her eyes shaded by her right hand.

"I won."

Just as we hugged Marie came out with the phone.

"Dad," she whispered. "It's them and you're on the speaker so be careful what you say."

It was the current bishop, Bob Johnson. "Porter, I am here at our Convention and pleased to tell you that you are to be the sixth bishop of the

Diocese of Western North Carolina. Would you like to say hello to your people?"

I stared across the street into the deep woods of a vacant lot. "Well, first I'm overwhelmed," I said. "Second, I am grateful to you for your trust in me. I hope to be a bishop for all people and sincerely devote myself to find unity through the Holy Spirit."

I heard applause from the other end. Then I said, "You know I hope Thomas Wolfe was wrong," but the call was abruptly cut off. I said, "You can go home again," to a dead line.

Before I could put the phone down, it rang again. The call was from one of my parishioners at St. Gregory's. "I am trying to be happy for you," she said, "but I am not. I never thought you'd leave."

The phone rang again. "Porter, this is Frank Griswold."

I almost said, "Holy shit" but I caught myself. "Presiding Bishop Griswold. What an honor." It was like talking to the Queen of England. Frank Griswold was the head of the entire Episcopal Church.

"You can call me Frank now. We are going to work together."

"Well, thank you Presiding Bishop. You know, I am a huge fan of yours." Then I realized I was being a teenager. "I am looking forward to all of this."

"Well. Welcome to the House."

I had no idea what he was talking about. Was he asking me to stay with him? "Excuse me?"

"The House of Bishops. You are part of that now."

"Oh," I said. I still didn't know what the House meant, and I wondered what else I was now a part of.

We heard from all my family and Jo's family and every priest I had ever known, most of my parish, and a slew of bishops I had never heard of. The battery for the kitchen phone ran out and then after a few hours the battery for Jo's office phone ran out. At six o'clock the house was finally still.

We sat at the kitchen table drinking peppermint tea.

"Are you happy?" Jo asked.

"I am everything," I said. "Happy, scared, excited, bewildered, disoriented. You?"

"Trying to be happy for you, but not sure what it means for the rest of us. How long is this for?"

I looked at her as if she had asked if the world was flat. "Forever," I said. "There's no place else to go."

"Holy shit."

# 7

# The House of Bishops

When you are doing the sort of work you have taken on, essentially an
apostolic work, you may have to face the fact that your work will be apparently
worthless and even achieve no result at all . . . As you get used to this idea
you start more and more to concentrate not on the results but on the value,
the rightness, the truth of the work itself . . . In the end . . . it is the reality of
personal relationships that saves everything

—THOMAS MERTON, *THE HIDDEN GROUND OF LOVE: THE
LETTERS OF THOMAS MERTON ON RELIGIOUS EXPERIENCE
AND SOCIAL CONCERNS*

"YOU DON'T KNOW WHAT you've gotten yourself into, do you?"

I shook my head and said, "Not a clue."

I stared at the man with a square jaw, dressed in a crisp blue blazer, and
his kind wife as they sat on our leather sunroom sofa. How had this come
to pass?

Two weeks earlier, on Saturday May 1, 2004 at one o'clock in the afternoon I was elected to be the sixth bishop of the Episcopal Diocese of
Western North Carolina. In the days that followed the election, I received
letters in my Athens, Georgia mailbox from people I did not know, welcoming me to "The House." The return addresses were places not in our address
book: St. Louis, Omaha, Miami. I supposed they were bishops because the
envelopes had "Rt. Rev." before their names. Why were they writing me?

The man was the Presiding Bishop's Assistant for Pastoral Care. He was also a bishop who had the job of training new bishops and giving them a clue about what they had gotten into. He was tall and solid. His square jaw made him look like an ex-football player. He had wide shoulders and an athletic spring in his step. His wife was at least a foot shorter.

We sat in the sunroom of our brick ranch house, our visitors on the couch, and Jo and I in armchairs flanking our fireplace. I looked around the room to make sure we had successfully picked up our teenage daughter's detritus—notebooks, Diet Coke cans, textbooks with crisp clean spines that made me wonder if they had been opened. Dressed in his blue blazer, the bishop sat with a two-inch-thick white notebook on his lap and looked very professional.

"We are here to welcome Porter to the House of Bishops and Jo to the Community of Bishop Spouses," the bishop announced. Rising, he gave me the notebook.

"What's this?" I asked.

"It's your new life," he said with a little laugh as if he were letting me in on a deep secret.

"What do you mean, 'new life'?" I asked, my voice louder than I intended. I could feel Jo stiffen next to me. "I am taking a new job in the church, but I don't need a new life. I have one."

The bishop's wife coughed. Jo's hand gripped my leg.

"That's why we are here," he said in a calming voice. "To help your transition into this new life of being a bishop. Becoming a bishop is like going from being a lawyer to being a judge. It's not just scope or degree; it's kind as well."

He paused, but Jo and I didn't say anything.

His wife said, "Don't worry. The bishops who get in trouble are the ones who think they know everything."

"Well, that's not me," I said. "When you talk about the House of Bishops, I don't even know what house you are talking about."

"The community of bishops is called the House of Bishops. It includes all the bishops in The Episcopal Church."

"How many bishops are there?" Jo asked.

"Well," there are one hundred and ten dioceses, so there's at least one from each of those, but some have assistant bishops so there are probably a hundred and thirty. We get together twice a year—in the fall and spring."

His wife looked at Jo and me and said, "I know it's overwhelming, but the good news is, your friends will be other bishops and their spouses because they're the only people you can talk to about what you will do. They're the only ones who will understand the mess you have to deal with and the secrets you have to keep."

Jo and I still were dumbfounded sitting there staring at these two people bringing us news that wasn't expected. After a moment, the bishop continued, "Remember, from now on there are no private conversations you can have apart from other bishops. You should assume that everything you say will be public regardless of how many promises people make about confidentiality."

Jo and I nudged each other. Since the Saturday of the election, the wave of excitement from the envisioned new life was slipping away drip by drip.

He pointed to the notebook. "There's all kind of information here, but the main thing is your calendar which is in the front."

"What do you mean? How could you have my calendar?"

He chuckled. "Just read it, and it will make sense. You are part of something way bigger than before." When I didn't say anything, he went on. "There are the two bishop meetings a year as I mentioned, plus you'll have the College for Bishops that meets for a week for three years, plus there's our General Convention every three years and committee meetings. You and the airlines are going to be friends whether you want to be or not."

That night Jo and I sat in our bed with the fat notebook open and went over our new calendar. I was to be ordained bishop September 18 in Asheville, but three days later I was to be in Spokane, Washington for the Fall House of Bishops meeting. I glanced at her and saw the line of her lips harden before she spoke.

"You said there wasn't much travel to this job. You remember you have a daughter in high school, right? And a son who still needs you even though he's in college. Looks like I am holding the bag while you fly all over doing this bishop thing. This isn't a bait and switch, is it?"

"Honest to God," I said. "I don't know what it is."

* * *

When I was in college, I read a small book by D.H. Lawrence called *Classic Studies in American Literature*. When I finished reading it, I turned to the front and read it again. I had never encountered anything like it—funny, erudite, conversational, insightful, irreverent—so not me. However, when I got to the chapter on Edgar Allan Poe, a paragraph burned in my brain, and I knew Poe's struggle was my struggle too:

"The central law of all organic life is that each organism is intrinsically isolate and single in itself. The moment its isolation breaks down, and there comes an actual mixing and confusion, death sets in . . . But the secondary law of all organic life is that each organism only lives through contact with other matter, assimilation, and contact with other life . . . "[1]

If we get too close to other people, we die. If we get too far away from other people, we die. My life had been an unsuccessful search for a balance. Of the two ways of dying, I had primarily feared getting too close to people. I was not a hermit, nor a recluse, nor incapable of conversation or even friendship. But using Lawrence's terms, I maintained a firm envelope around myself to avoid any "mixing and confusion." As an adult I could say I was an "introvert," but that convenient label glossed over the pain. Yes, I did not mix with people as well as my brother or sister, but this wasn't about temperament or introversion; it was a mode of survival. I knew that withdrawal led to a death, but by and large I preferred it to the death of assimilation because I could control the pain.

In Atlanta I had a therapist who said, "Why is it you are still putting pelts on your wall? Who are you trying to impress?"

I didn't know how to answer, but I knew it was true.

She went on to say, "Let the people who love you love you just because you are you." After a pause she added, "Here's the thing. People can't get enough of what they don't need. So, for you, no more prizes to impress others."

Was this bishop thing just another prize, another pelt on my wall?

As I thumbed through the fat notebook the morning after the Presiding Bishop Assistant's visit, I wondered "Why did I do this?" Yes, I was restless after nine years of being the rector of the local Episcopal Church in Athens, Georgia, but why was I always restless? Did I really think that the House of Bishops could or would be a home?

\* \* \*

Tuesday September 20, 2004, three days after I was ordained the Bishop of Western North Carolina, I walked into the Davenport Hotel in Spokane. The lobby looked like Grand Central Station—a vast open space with pockets of brown lush easy chairs in clusters. "Looks like bishops don't stay in Motel Sixes," I thought. I didn't know what the dress code was, so I played it safe with my blue blazer and charcoal gray pants. After being ordained for eleven years, I only owned two ties—red and blue. Since I was trying to blend in, I opted for blue.

---

1. Lawrence, "Edgar Allan Poe," 47.

When I walked into the meeting room a few hours later, I saw the Presiding Bishop—the person elected to be the head of all the bishops and the head of The Episcopal Church—standing by the podium. He was supposed to have come to Asheville to ordain me but backed out two days before the event because he was afraid he couldn't get home since the weather in Asheville was iffy with Hurricane Ivan.

We shook hands and he said in his cultured voice, "Sorry about last weekend, but I just couldn't take a chance on getting stuck."

I tried not to take offense at the notion that being detained in Asheville was "being stuck," but I could feel the blood coming to my face. It started an old tape of fearing I was ignored.

"It's all right Presiding Bishop. I'm happy to be here."

"Porter, we're all bishops here. Just use my first name."

Then he turned and called to his assistant, a heavyset man standing behind him, "Where's that Bible and present for Porter Taylor?"

The man was dressed in a black suit and black clergy shirt and collar. Without a word, he handed two wrapped boxes, one larger than the other, to the Presiding Bishop.

"This is the Bible, and this is a small gift to help you stay grounded."

"Thank you, Presiding Bishop," I said, and then realized I had not used his first name as directed.

That night in my hotel room I opened the smaller package and found a framed quote by St. Augustine. "For you I am a bishop, but with you I am a Christian: one is an office, accepted, the other is a gift, received. One is danger, the other is safety. If I am happier to be redeemed with you, than to be placed over you, then I shall as the Lord commanded be more fully your Servant."[2]

The more I read it, the less I understood it. One is danger, the other is safety. Was there always a gap between *with you* and *for you*, *bishop* and *Christian*, *accepted* and *received*? Did bishops need a separate house to protect themselves from the danger, and if so, then how is it that they connect with others? The luxurious hotel was the first clue that this House of Bishops may be luxurious but had very thick walls.

The next morning when I walked into the hotel ballroom for our first meeting, I discovered all the tables had numbers and each bishop was assigned to a specific table: eight seats at each circular table. At the meeting of the bishops in 1991 in Phoenix, the bishops behaved so badly—screaming at each other, calling one another names, behaving very unepiscopal—the then Presiding Bishop Edmund Browning brought in a consultant who

2. St. Augustine, "On the Anniversary of His Ordination," 292–94.

suggested changing the seating chart. Up to then, bishops sat in rows in order of seniority. The newer bishops never got to speak because the old farts in the front stood up and pontificated.

I was at table twelve. "God is not good," I said to myself as I sat down. The only vacant seat was next to the bishop who ordained me to the priesthood. I knew he thought I was too liberal to go very far in that diocese. When I asked about making a move to another church, he said, "There's no place for you in this diocese." I heard that he did not vote to affirm my election to be the Bishop of Western North Carolina. This wasn't the seat I would have chosen, but this is where I was.

To my surprise, the first speaker was Richard Rodriguez, the writer and sometimes correspondent on the PBS NewsHour. He was slender and dressed in a white shirt and tan pants. He looked simply elegant.

"The world is getting brown," he said. "Children take crayons and put them on the sidewalk in the sun and they all melt and become brown. Brown is a color we're afraid of; we can't deal with brown. There are more than three hundred words in Brazilian Portuguese for brown. In America, we are between white and black. The history of our nation and of the world is filled with stories about brown."

Rodriguez was engaging and funny and stimulating. *If this is being a bishop, I am all in.*

The meeting was four days long. The business sessions were all downhill after Richard Rodriguez.

This meeting was a year after the ordination of Gene Robinson, the first gay person to be ordained a bishop. The conservatives' nerves were still raw. Each day before lunch, the business adjourned, and we had the Holy Eucharist (the Lord's Supper). As we were moving toward the worship space, I noticed about ten bishops walking to the parking lot.

"What's that about?" I asked my new friend from Kentucky.

"Oh, those are our conservative bishops who are much too pure to be polluted by worshiping with us sinners who let gays into the House of Bishops," he said.

It was my first clue that the House of Bishops was not a completely harmonious home. Maybe Richard Rodriguez wasn't right after all. In this house the colors weren't mixing together.

* * *

When I was eight years old, some friends at school asked me to join the YMCA Indian Guides. "It's cool," they told me. "We take campouts and learn about smoke signals and stuff."

"But," one of them added, "you have to bring your dad."

Two weeks later my dad drove me to a one-story white wooden house on the other side of Asheville. There were about ten pairs of sons and fathers. When the meeting started, we sat in a circle, sons sitting next to their fathers. The boys who had been there before wore a leather cord around their heads with a feather sticking up in the back. The leader was one of the dads. He talked about this being a fellowship and how in this circle dads were just like their sons, only more experienced.

"Here, your dad's not your dad," he said. "He's your buddy."

When we were walking to the car, my father laid his hand on my head and said, "Granville. Listen to me. I am not your buddy. I am your father."

We never went back to the Indian Guides.

* * *

Growing up I wondered about the emotional economy in the Taylor household. In a world of limited resources, like affection or blessing or deep love, sometimes I thought there wasn't enough for a person to offer any of these to more than one person at a time. I never thought of my parents as mean or unkind people. I loved them in my childhood way, and I knew they told me they loved me.

However, my sense of emotional economy was that adults had enough goodness and protection to share with one person in the world. I was a preemie. I only weighed two and half pounds at birth and therefore, was a month in the hospital in an incubator. My twin sister went home in two weeks.

When I was taken from Piedmont Hospital in Rock Hill, South Carolina, I intuitively knew that just as when you are late for recess, the teams are already chosen. The two Sarahs, my mother and sister, were paired and the two Richards, my father and brother, were paired. I was born the odd one out. There were no villains in this story. My parents didn't beat or belittle me. I probably had emotional needs they never could understand. Sometimes I felt like a foreign exchange student in my own family. At some point I got over blame. It wasn't a question of love in the house. It was simple economics. There was love, but for whatever reason, I wasn't able to let it sink all the way into me.

I accommodated. Until I was fifteen, my brother was bigger. My sister was always sweeter and chattier than me. Sometimes I felt like the runt in the litter trying to get to the bread of life but was stuck circling the bowl.

The love drive finds a way to connection. We lived in a two-story house. Four bedrooms upstairs with two baths. The baths were divided according to gender. The men's bathroom had the bonus of a walk-in shower. It was made with white octagonal tiles and was so long that there was an opening instead of a door. In the morning my dad would shower after getting his coffee. When I was about five, I would hear him coming up the stairs from the kitchen. I'd lie in bed listening for the shower to start.

When I heard the water, I'd slip out of bed and tiptoe across the room, so I wouldn't wake my brother. I'd go into the men's bathroom and sit on the floor just at the opening for the shower. The hot spray bathed my face and moistened my pajama shirt and I'd put my hands on my head in a gesture of self-blessing. When I closed my eyes and leaned against the wall, the wet warmth, I was home.

How could I find that sense of belonging in the bishops' house?

* * *

The next House of Bishops meeting was at Camp Allen, Texas, about an hour and a half north of Houston. It's Texas—big, sandy, and plain. This meeting was much more casual; bishops wore blue jeans and T-shirts. I began to relax because I knew a few people and had a general idea of the meeting's flow. No spouses came to the spring meeting. Since there were only twelve female bishops, this had a boys' club feel. At night, a crowd played poker and drank scotch. Another group watched March Madness. I looked for a book club but finding none retreated to my room.

Our meetings were in a large, windowless basement room—again with our round tables. I was still stuck with the Tennessee bishop, but I was determined to make the best of it. We could listen to each other, or we could ignore each other. At the tables we didn't argue; we simply said what we thought. Because bishops have no jurisdiction outside their diocese, we are all equals.

The first few days were filled with people coming in to give us reports about activities around the church. Most reports did not seem worth the time and money to fly someone into Texas to talk for twenty minutes about a new program on evangelism or Christian Formation or the plight of our seminaries. As I looked around the room, most of the bishops were staring at their computer screens, not at the speakers.

Every day began with a church service: prayers, sermon, the Lord's Supper. Two chaplains are assigned to be in charge of worship, so the bishops don't get competitive about who can do liturgy the best. A monk from an Episcopal monastery in Boston was my favorite. His sermons were funny but always had a story that kept repeating in my head as I sat through the long business sessions. During our business sessions he would sit in the back of the hall, wearing his black monk's robe, often fingering his rosary beads as the speakers droned on and on. In some ways he was my assurance that our doorway into the holy was open despite the drudgery of our work.

The last day was a business meeting. I can't go into any details because one of our oaths is to let the formal report speak for the meeting. However, what I can communicate is that I learned that the Southern tendency to whitewash conflict doesn't work in the long run. It doesn't help to pretend, "We are all saying the same thing" when indeed we are not. There was what can be called a fierce conversation over activities of a conservative bishop before a worldwide meeting of the Presiding Bishops in Ireland. The Anglican Church in Africa has always been more conservative around issues of human sexuality. There was a charge that one of our bishops counselled with some of the African bishops before the meeting.

What I learned that day is that leadership involves telling the truth and accepting the repercussions. The meeting was tense. Some bishops engaged in fierce conversations, and their engagement alerted me to the fact that being a bishop is more than getting one's own diocese to work. In the bishop's ordination process we pledge to "share with your fellow bishops in the government of the whole Church,"[3] but I didn't realize that governing could mean calling one another to account. The truth telling that day opened my eyes to the divisions in the church and made me wonder what my role would be in the future to confront those or even be confronted. I thought I had enough to do just figuring out how to lead in Western North Carolina, but clearly this vocation was wider and deeper than my conception.

However, the meeting ended up being uplifting. One of the progressive bishops came to one of the microphones on the floor and said, "Let us be fair and let us be true to one another." He paused and looked around the room, his shaggy beard making him look very Old Testament. "The Primates have said we should not ordain any more gays or lesbians as bishops until our General Convention in 2006 votes on this. Therefore, I move that we have a moratorium on ordaining any bishops until then. If one member of the body suffers, we all suffer."

3. *Book of Common Prayer*, 518.

When he sat down, there was a silence across the room. For me, it was a deep moment, a moment when some door in a dark place opens and invites everyone into a new place in the sun. The earlier acrimonious exchange sickened me and unraveled my enthusiasm for this ministry. I didn't want to be a resident in a house of lies and acrimony. But this was a different place because it meant we would do more than talk about what was right; we would do something right. Instead of only telling our gay and lesbian brothers and sisters to wait, we would all wait.

When the Presiding Bishop asked, "All those in favor?" the room echoed with "Aye."

I called Jo that night to give her my daily report.

"How was your day?" she asked.

"Turbulent," I replied. I didn't know what else to say because it was so complicated. I knew what I felt but had few words that could capture it.

"Bam?" she prompted.

"Jo, this job is not going to be what we thought. It's way bigger and way messier. I can tell there's a lot I won't like because I already don't like it. I don't know if I'll be very effective, but I do know it will push me. It might make me come out and show my colors in a way I've never had to do before. I mean, we vote on hard things, and you have to say 'yes' or 'no' even when you don't really understand anything."

After a pause, she said, "Did you do that today?"

"Yes, I did."

"And are you proud of how you voted."

"Yes, I am."

"Then I am proud of you, Bam." After another pause, she added, "But I am sick of you giving more time to the bishops than to me and the kids and I'm ready for you to come back. The leaves on the Lenten rose have come out. I need you to help me prepare the garden."

"Believe me, I can't wait to be home."

# 8

# Passage to India

Above all it is the Love which created and sustains the world, which is revealed
not as a person standing over against the world, but as the Communion of
Love which embraces all humanity and all creation and is the Wisdom which
orders the universe, for Wisdom is Knowledge by love.

—BEDE GRIFFITHS, *UNIVERSAL WISDOM*

FIRST THE SMELLS. DIESEL, food, sheer humanity, cow dung, smoke from
small fires even in the city.

Then, the noise. Horns. Always car horns. Long blasts. High-pitched
bursts. As if you were lost in a percussion unit before class begins.

What mattered were the faces. I stepped out of the Kolkata airport
with Susan, my traveling companion who was a laywoman from the diocese.
I felt like a rock star coming out on the stage. Eight o'clock in the morning
and hundreds of people stood at the exit doors—waving, shouting, some
with signs, and children jumping up and down.

Four steps beyond the door we were surrounded by men offering help.
"Carry your bags?" "Taxi?" Since this was my fourth trip here, instead of
becoming flustered, I relaxed and was even relieved to be away from my
button-down rule-driven world in the West.

I came to Kolkata because the Diocese of Western North Carolina had
a companion relationship with the Diocese of Durgapur. Both are in the
Anglican Communion and share a common way of being church. When I

first became bishop, I wanted a companion relationship and sent a blanket email around the world—seeking a companion. Within six hours the bishop responded. After my visit in 2006 we entered an official relationship. I visited again in 2008 and 2010.

"Porter." In the sea of faces I saw the bishop's assistant waving.

Durgapur is three hours north of Kolkata. Because it's a steel town, few tourists come there. If you flipped a manhole cover in the average American city, it came from Durgapur. Because the factory was fueled by coal, there was a haze that never went away. After a few days, your clothes retained a harsh metallic smell.

In the car, I wasn't thinking about that. I was thinking about the strangeness of India as we passed by. The trucks with bright-colored signs painted on the backs that said, "Please blow horn." The houses with straw roofs. The cows in the street with their horns painted red and yellow. Signs saying "Hindu Hotel" in front of one-room buildings. The Indian stare that made the world stop for a moment. The fires by the side of the road. The roadside stall with a man sitting behind a sewing machine, waiting for customers. The shrill noise. The music with no melody. All of it.

I came here for an "official visit." The Indian bishop asked me to preside at their Convention worship service. Each day of my schedule was filled with a meeting with some organization. Those events were my justification for coming, but not the reason. I came to get out of my sanitized stuck self. I came for the tonic of India to cure me from my sanitized life. I came because I had forgotten why I wanted to be, or should be, a bishop.

He and I were both ordained bishops in 2004. When he was ordained, he discovered there was no office, no employees, no diocesan ministries. There was just him. When I first visited him in 2006, his diocese had purchased a compound with a house for the bishop and guest quarters. We ate our meals with the bishop and his wife in the dining room of their house.

When I returned in 2008, there was a dining hall for guests. When I visited in 2010, there were two dormitories for thirty children. When I asked the bishop about it, he said, "Across the street was a slum village. Families lived in shacks made from tin pieces or plastic sheets and mud walls. But the government wanted the property, so one morning bulldozers came and leveled the village. We took in the children because otherwise they wouldn't be able to go to school."

As I got out of the car, I saw an office building and a cathedral. What had I done in my ten years? How many children could we have housed with the right will and imagination?

The diocese had built a two-story guest building. Every building in this part of India is made of concrete—walls, floor, ceiling. My room was narrow. Two twin beds filled the space. The bathroom was blue tiled, with two buckets under a spout. I lay down to recover from the twenty-two-hour trip, but the sounds of children playing in the courtyard through the open window kept me from sleeping.

That night the diocese held a dinner for Susan and me at the school next door. We stepped through an arc of orange bougainvillea into a garden decorated with Christmas lights. People lined to greet me as if I were the Queen of England. "Bishop Porter, thank you for coming." "We missed you last year." "How is your wife?"

A young woman in a deep crimson sari took my hand.

I said, "I am so glad to see you again."

She took my hand but did not let go. "Bishop, we are so glad to see you because we have missed you." Her voice dropped and she took a breath to compose herself. She looked me in the eye and said in a strong voice, "Why have you stayed away from us?"

My breath stopped. Had I hurt these people because I became overwhelmed with my work for three years? Did I miss something about friendship?

"I am so sorry," I said. "I couldn't come because I have been fundraising and could not get away. But it's not because of you. I pray for you every morning. I do. And our relationship is important to me and the diocese. I promise."

As I spoke, she kept her gaze but softened. She breathed. A smile came to her face. "Good," she said, and waggled her head. "You are very important to us as well, and we miss you."

My frantic pace in the last handful of years had moved me to a survival mode. At home I had focused on my to-do list instead of what this encounter meant. The Companion Diocese had become another duty. I had become the empty suit I used to talk about—the guy who looks over your shoulder for someone more important to talk to.

"I love being here and our companionship is close to my heart."

"Good," she said in her soft voice. "You are close to our heart." She paused and patted my chest with her palm. "Come, we have prepared a banquet for you."

We were served spicy chicken, rice and dal, curries, pan, and ice cream for dessert. The meal must have cost the diocese a fortune.

In a typical India non sequitur, the background music was The Rolling Stones. As we ate in this lovely garden, I heard Mick Jagger warn, "Rape, murder, it's just a kiss away."

Of course, they gave us presents. Since this was my fourth trip, I was beyond surprise. The bishop's assistant called my traveling companion and me forward. First one of the women leaders put a string of marigolds over each of our heads. I had to lean down for her to reach me. Then the assistant announced, "This is for our good friend Bishop Porter," and handed me a large flat box wrapped in shiny red paper. It was a faux leather briefcase; handy but hard to fit into my luggage. And I got a notebook cover and a wallet. It was not the thought that counted; it was my showing up that counted.

In return, I gave the bishop a Cross pen and his wife earrings that Jo had tastefully picked out.

* * *

I don't worry about sleep in India. I awoke at three o'clock and read and dozed until I heard the sound of shoes slapping on the driveway and a muffled sound of violins playing off-key.

I looked out my second-story window and saw boys, probably twelve years old, running laps around the dormitory. It was seven o'clock, an hour and a half before their school started, but they were dressed in their uniforms—red checked shirts, blue tie, and blue pants—jogging together, laughing, talking, being twelve.

I dressed in what had become my India uniform—khakis and purple shirt and blue blazer—and walked over to the compound. The boys were now kicking a soccer ball back and forth.

"Good morning, sir," they exclaimed in high-pitched prepubescent voices.

I found the source of the music and looked in. Twelve students—anywhere from twelve to eighteen years old—stood with their violins perpendicular, facing a large woman waving her arms like she was in an aerobics class.

Their eyes were fixed on the teacher as if this were life or death. Each wore a blue-and-red school uniform. They were playing "Amazing Grace" slowly and with screeches. They stared at their music and then shot glances at the conductor as if this music were their whole world.

She was a stocky woman, wearing a rumpled light-blue dress that came to her midcalf. Her hair was stringy and didn't look clean.

Suddenly she stood up straight and declared, "Right. Off you go. Breakfast and then school. Don't forget we practice again after supper."

As the children filed out, each said to me in the same high voice, "Good morning, sir." I nodded and murmured, "Good morning."

"I'm Porter Taylor," I said to the teacher.

"You must be the American bishop." She extended her hand to shake in a firm grip. "I've been here for two years shaping up the children." I wondered if I would ever have that kind of focus, which would mean letting go of everything in my blurred, crammed life.

\* \* \*

A year before this trip, the head of The Episcopal Church, Katharine Jefferts Schori, came to our diocese to be our keynote speaker for a conference on outreach programs. We met at our conference center set in the Pisgah National Forest. I had planned a Saturday afternoon session for the various justice organizations to present their activities as a kind of fair—or "Aren't We Wonderful?" presentation. A deacon in the diocese was to talk about our companion relationship with Durgapur. I assumed she would talk about the schools and the clinics. Same old same old, but new to the Presiding Bishop.

No—she went to the mic and said, "It's time we did something about the evil of human trafficking, and we are—our diocese with the Diocese of Durgapur. India leads the world in the sex slave trade, and we are going to be part of the solution."

The Presiding Bishop said, "Wonderful." I didn't say anything because I didn't know anything about it.

This was why my fellow traveler was in Durgapur. She had helped to establish a safe house in the northern part of the diocese—just on the border of Bangladesh. The photo I saw was a small square brown building that blended into the Indian dirt. The women were sheltered, fed, and eventually moved south where there were jobs and a new life. She was here because the safe house was funded by the sale of scarves sewn here on the compound back in the USA.

On our many flights to get here she told me that hearing about getting girls out of trafficking had been a conversion for her. We sat beside each other in the flight from New York to Dubai. She had wrapped the blue Air Emirates blanket around her and used her eye mask to hold back her long brown hair. I wondered why a fiftyish mother of two teenagers was traveling to India. About two hours into our flight across the Atlantic, she told me.

"I was a mother of two girls and ran a clothing store in a small town until I heard a talk about trafficking. A voice in my head said, I have to be part of that." As she spoke, the light airy voice I'd heard before left her. She twisted to look me straight on and said in a deeper tone, "This is my life now."

One afternoon I was standing in the Durgapur compound. She walked up to me with a smiling girl dressed in her school uniform. My fellow traveler had her arm on the girl's shoulder. "Porter, this is Gita. She is from Malta."

The girl smiled and held her right hand up as a wave that reminded me of someone taking an oath.

"I am glad to see you, Gita. What grade are you in?"

She didn't answer but turned to my companion traveler with a questioning look. "Go on to the sewing center, Gita. I'll see you later," my companion said, patting the girl on the shoulder.

After the girl departed, I raised my eyebrows. Dressed in a kind of red knee-length tunic and billowing blue pants, she smiled at me.

"Gita is one of the girls we rescued. She's fourteen. She's too ashamed to go to school so she sews with the other women."

"Oh, dear God," I said. "How is she?" I was fumbling because I felt not only stupid but a wave of sadness. It seemed that a darkness had come into what I thought was a place set apart.

"Gita is happy," she said. "The other kids like her. It's the first time she's belonged to anything in years. And she's safe. She can sleep at night."

That afternoon I gazed over the garden outside my bedroom, thinking about Gita and thinking about me. In his ten years, the Indian bishop had started schools, built medical clinics, and constructed a cathedral. But most of all, he had rescued children from evil. In my time, I had kept up with my emails, avoided making many people angry, kept the diocese in the black, and enabled the church machine to keep running. All my sins were sins of omission not commission, but they weighed on me.

I felt as if I had let my moment run through my fingers. Ten years as bishop and what? Of course, I had plenty of excuses—the economic downturn, a small diocese, a deep hierarchical suspicion—but nowhere near the excuses the Indians had.

I thought about the two women from Hendersonville, North Carolina, who found a way to save girls halfway around the world from slavery. I remembered when I heard one of them speak that day at Lake Logan. My head wondered, "Where in the world did this come from? Did she go through the right committees? Did our finance commission agree to any of this?" But my heart went deeper into a soft place I had not visited in a long time. "Yes, yes, yes," I said to myself. "This is the work of the church."

As I looked at the flowers, I didn't see the flowers, I saw the Indian girl's round smiling face. I saw her red-checked blouse and dark blue skirt—just like all the other children. She was now part of something good.

I wondered if my moment had passed. Did I have a second act?

* * *

Jo and I had talked about what to bring to the Indian children. There were thirty of them, so it had to be small. T-shirts, balls, bracelets? Finally, Jo said, "Pencils. Colored pencils. I'll order them from the Dick Blick Catalog. They'll be right for any age." They were the right gift, but they also weighed ten pounds—eight pencils per pack—forty packs.

Monday afternoon the children were playing in the compound, and I brought the box down. A volunteer gathered the children, all wearing their uniforms. I handed the packs of pencils out one by one. "Thank you, sir," each said. I realized they probably didn't own anything. The school next door didn't give them books. The teacher wrote on the board and the students wrote it down. A few of the six-year-olds stared at their new prize. Then they all jumped up and waved them around.

One of our projects was to get sponsors for the children. Two hundred and fifty dollars paid for food, uniforms, and supplies for a year.

Jo and I sponsored a six-year-old girl. I met her on pencil day. It was a cool day by Indian standards, so she wore a shawl around her head. She was tiny and barely came to my belt buckle. She spoke almost no English.

Jo and I had two gifts for her. First was a kaleidoscope. When she first looked through it, she thrust it from her eye and stared at me. I guided her hands back to her face and showed her how to turn the cylinder to make new configurations of color and light. Her eyes grew wide, and she laughed. Then she ran to show the other children but would only let one use it before she took it back to look again to see if it still worked.

After a while she came back to where I sat. I gave her the second present—an inflatable plastic globe. The girl had no idea what this was. The other children had formed a ring around us, wondering as well. I had to inflate the globe breath by breath. One of the children offered to help but my hypervigilance about hygiene wouldn't let me accept. When it was done, I pointed to India and to the girl and then to the US and then pointed to me. Ruth, the English woman, helped them understand.

But really, they didn't care. It was a big ball to them. They played a new version of volleyball with it—laughing and yelling, running in circles—the world kept afloat in the air by the small brown hands.

I forgot why I came until I got here. That forgetfulness kept me away for three years. Why? *It's so I can help the bishop or promote the new initiatives. It's so I can help make a difference through the schools or clinics we support.* All that was true. But I went to India to thaw my heart and to catch a glimpse of what thanksgiving looks like. Yes, the Indians had cares as we did, but here in this place there wasn't the current of anxiety that ran my world. In spite of the enormous challenges, there was an ability to rejoice in the present, which I had forgotten but remembered when I saw the children bounce the world around in the air.

* * *

We ate our meals in the refectory on the compound. There was good news and bad news about the food. In my past visits I have stayed well. That was the good news. The bad news was that the same menu was served every day. Breakfast was cereal and one hard-boiled egg. Lunch was rice and dal. Dinner was rice and dal with chicken. Day after day. The only variation was in the amount of chutney I used.

Bishop Dutta invited representatives for a Thanksgiving Service from the various churches around the world that helped the diocese. In addition to Lisa and me, there were two couples from New Zealand, six people from various churches in Charleston, South Carolina, and one young man from Australia.

I knew one couple from Charleston because they had lived in our diocese before moving. The doctor and his wife had been instrumental in setting up the medical clinic in the compound. They had been coming to Durgapur every year since 2007. However, this year they came to conduct healing ministries throughout the diocese. "We had two thousand people in Purulia," he told me. "The service was three hours."

That night at dinner I sat across from a round-faced woman from Charleston. I liked her laugh.

"Do you go to the same church as the doctor in Charleston?" I asked her.

She looked down at her plate. I didn't know what I had said wrong. In the silence I stared at the mango chutney in between us.

"I go to St. Michael's," she said.

"Oh, I hear it's a great church," I said. We both stared at the chutney.

St. Michael's is one of the parishes in Charleston that left The Episcopal Church over their disapproval of our ordaining gays and lesbians. I was on the committee to help the remaining Episcopalians in Charleston, and therefore, I knew how acrimonious the arguments were. One woman on the committee told me, "When I see old friends in the grocery store that have left our church, I just turn around and go the other way. It's too painful."

Susan looked at me and said, "We are having a healing service tonight over in the Cathedral. Why don't you come?"

"Sure. I'd love to."

The place was packed. I arrived late on purpose because I didn't want to be involved in the service. I knew the church the doctor had joined was charismatic and very conservative. I wasn't so much keeping my liberalism pure as I didn't want to mess up what they were doing. During my first visit to India, I asked the Indian bishop if there was any problem with The Episcopal Church's liberal stance on human sexuality, and he said, "Porter, we are a big country and we have too many problems to worry about what you are doing in America." But the other Americans would worry about what I had been doing.

The service went on for a long time. The priest in charge was one of the New Zealanders. His sermon was a list of Bible quotations intended to prove that Satan caused illnesses and that Jesus cured them. The hymns were what I called campfire songs, such as "Have You Seen Jesus My Lord?" Peppy but no depth. People waved their arms as they sang. I stood in the back row—a stiff white bishop.

Then there was the laying on of hands. In the front the healers were groups of three, mixed with Anglos and Indians. People would come up and the healers would lay their hands on them, and one of them would lean in and talk to the person.

I had done healing services hundreds of times as a priest, but of course, in the proper, emotionally closed Episcopal way. I asked the person what their petition was and then used the sentence from the prayer book: "I lay my hands upon you and anoint you with oil in the Name of our Lord and Savior Jesus Christ, beseeching him to uphold you and fill you with his grace, that you may know the healing power of his love. *Amen.*"[1] It was polite, controlled, and within our Episcopal decorum.

Here people fainted. Some cried out "Thank you Jesus" or some words in Bengali that I couldn't translate. Most cried after the laying on of hands.

I watched the trios. When a person came up, they leaned in and spoke and nodded their heads. Then they draped their arms around the person. As the middle leader laid hands on the person's head, the other two embraced the person in a cocoon.

I could see the doctor rock from side to side as he put his hands on each person's head. He'd lean in and speak in their ear. People wept. Women touched his feet when he was through. It wasn't dignified, but it was real. My spirituality was so refined and so precious that I didn't know what to do with such an earthy display of compassion. My focus on Centering Prayer, the Enneagram, the Daily Office—there was something antiseptic compared to this raw human contact of hands to heads. There seemed to be a language

---

1. *Book of Common Prayer*, 456.

of need and hurt that went beyond dialects. I wondered why I was sitting in my sanitized seat on the back row.

At the very end I went forward. One of the Indians directed me to the right side, and I ended up facing one of the women from Charleston. Another woman from South Carolina stood to my right and an Indian priest was to my left. The Charleston woman leaned toward me, our heads almost touching. She put her two hands on my shoulders, and I realized how large a woman she was.

"I have had vertigo for five years. I seek healing."

"How does it ail you?"

"I am dizzy almost all of the time. In the morning sometimes I can't walk a straight line."

She put oil on her thumb and traced a cross on my forehead. She put her hands on my head and the others clutched my shoulders. I felt her fingers grip my skull.

She began talking in a low voice, "Lord, here's your servant Porter, a man of God, in need of your help. Lord, we just want you to send your Spirit on him, Lord. We just want you to take away the darkness around him, Lord. Just loosen Satan's grip on him, Lord. Because Lord we know he's your prayer warrior. Lord we know he's a man of God sent to do your work, Lord. Just free him, Lord. Make him stand up right, Lord. Get the devil far from him, Lord and heal him in Jesus' name."

As she talked, I felt her energy warm me and I felt myself wanting to be the person she believed I was—not so much a prayer warrior, but yes, a man of God. I realized I wanted to connect with the kind of power she described. I was tired of being the CEO of an institution. I wanted the current to run through me the way the healer, Susan, believed it ran through her and probably did run through her.

Here I was with my shoes off standing in a church in far east India asking for healing, but in that moment, I knew I was in the right place. Where could I ask for healing at home?

I hugged my healer and the other two persons. I felt lighter. I felt connected. I felt as if I had stepped out of being a foreigner and was just one of the many in this room in need.

As I returned to my chair in the back, I realized that here was probably the only place she or anyone else who had left The Episcopal Church in South Carolina and I could meet. It was too toxic in the Carolinas to talk about who was right or wrong and what was fair or unfair. But none of the arguments and anger had a home here. Here there was simply need and grace.

* * *

The primary reason the Indian bishop asked us to come was to attend the Thanksgiving Service. This is the Indian version of our diocesan convention, except it was much better because there were no votes or resolutions or business meetings. There were just dance performances, food, music, and church.

People began arriving on Friday. The bishop told me it took about ten hours by bus to get to Durgapur. The service Sunday was at nine o'clock. I had brought my vestments—white alb and gold cope with my white miter. Before the service all the guests were escorted to the gate of the compound where two rows of chairs stood. We sat and took off our shoes and socks.

Women dressed in green plaid saris knelt before us as we sat in chairs and washed our feet. The water was cold. When she finished, she stood and then stooped to touch her two hands to my feet. Then she backed up as she put her prayerful hands to her head. Each time, this had occurred and each time I was filled with too many feelings. I hated having a brown woman wash a white man's feet, and yet there was something truly cleansing about the experience. Being washed clean by someone who lived here seemed necessary for me to be ready to lead the worship—as if she were washing away all my suppositions and Western judgments so that I might come close to being present to whatever God would do. As if I had to let go and just receive, knowing it was not about what I wanted but what needed to be done.

Then the same women in green plaid put pots of flowers on their heads and began dancing a zigzag dance down the street toward the tent that was set for the thousands of people who had come. It was so India. The women with flowerpots were followed by twenty men with long skinny drums they beat with sticks. The men had a determined "don't mess with me, I'm a drummer" look. Then more women dancers wearing bright yellow saris did a dance that moved them all over the street—their arms outstretched as they twirled with each crossing of the road. Then the cross and candles, the clergy, and the Indian and me. Then the people. Two thousand people behind us. Talking, singing, laughing, clapping.

We gathered under a huge blue-and-red tent with rows and rows of chairs. When we reached the altar, the Indian bishop said, "Porter, you must preside. My shoulder is hurting me." My eyes grew wide. "I don't even know your prayer book."

"Don't worry," he said, "it's why we have books."

It was fine. Because their church and our church both come from the Church of England, the prayers were the same. I could have closed my eyes and done the service.

At communion, I was to help administer communion to the people. Their custom is for the clergy to dip the wafer into the wine and place it in the person's mouth. I worried about the hygiene of this for about thirty seconds and then realized, it's the body and blood of Christ and what germs could they get that they probably don't already have. And, it's India.

"The Body and Blood of Christ," I said over and over. The brown faces of men and women looked at me as they opened their mouths and stuck out their tongues.

"The Body and Blood of Christ" again and again and again. It became a mantra. For a moment I didn't care where I was. I was feeding and being fed. I was telling myself, "These people are the body and blood of Christ," right here right now.

For a moment I wasn't worried about my future. I wasn't filled with that burden of obligations, and I wasn't overwhelmed with any sense that I had not lived my life since becoming a bishop. Saying that sentence over and over was like taking an elevator to a deeper place—a place where my egocentric concerns vanished—my career, my accomplishments, my future. And I remembered it's about being fed and maybe it was as simple as showing up and opening your mouth to receive. Maybe all my angst was a diversion from the real work, which was admitting my hunger to belong and deep desire to make a difference. Maybe I should have stopped worrying about all that I had *not* done and all that did *not* happen and simply eat the bread before me. I did not know how to do this but looking at the swarm of Indians who had come with hands outstretched gave me the courage to go home and try.

# 9

# Lambeth 2008

So here is your vocation set out . . . It is your business to actualize within the
world of time and space . . . that more real life, that holy creative energy . . .
You shall work for mercy, order, beauty, significance.

—EVELYN UNDERHILL, *PRACTICAL MYSTICISM*

THE BUS STOPPED WITH a jolt. I looked out the front window and saw two
lanes of stalled cars and buses and trucks—a multicolored ribbon fading
into the Scotland hills. People stood beside their vehicles or walked in the
middle of the highway—talking, smoking, looking frustrated.

Jo and I were on a bus with twenty bishops and their spouses—half
American, half Scottish—traveling from Glasgow to Canterbury. After two
hours on the bus filled with laughter and church talk, we got stuck in this
standstill with no evident cause or culprit. We were on our way to the Lambeth Conference, a gathering of Anglican bishops and spouses from all over
the world, which happens every ten years. The non-British bishops were
invited to come a week early and enter the life of a parish. Jo and I were
lucky to be placed in a Scottish Episcopal Church in Alexandria, just outside Glasgow. Now the Scots and the visiting American bishops and spouses
were hopefully on their way to Canterbury.

"Anyone have whiskey?" came a Scottish voice from the back of the
bus. Someone else shouted, "Picnic time!"

In a few moments we sat on the highway guardrail, twenty bishops and wives, looking like tropical birds on a wire. It was July so the sleeves of our purple shirts were rolled up. Americans with baseball hats and Scots with proper hats with 360 bills. Scotch whiskey in paper cups, plastic bottles of orange juice, and biscuits passed up and down the rail.

Our fellow stranded travelers wandered over to see what was about. Some socialized; some quizzed us. It was all very properly Scottish—no questions about accepting Jesus as our personal savior.

"Are you a Yank?" "Will you see the queen?" "What's the archbishop going to do?"

I sat next to the Bishop of Glasgow whom Jo and I had gotten to know as we had been staying in his diocese. He was quieter than I but seemed more politically astute. He knew where the land mines were. One man came over, elderly, wearing a brown sweater and hat. Idris smiled and pushed his rimless glasses up his nose in a kind of Harry Truman pose as he greeted him. The man leaned toward Idris's face and said in a low growl, "Bishop, don't let the English bastards get you down."

He chuckled and gave him a pat on his arm. "Thanks, but it's not the English we're worried about."

\* \* \*

We arrived in Canterbury at two o'clock in the morning. The city was deserted. I stared out the window while most passengers slept. Jo's head rested on my shoulder. As the city streetlights flashed in the window I could see Jo's face. She looked like a child without concern for the changes and chances of the world. Our bus passed through gates with an arch that read The University of Kent. In a short time, we came to a stop in front of a short white woman who stood in the middle of the road dressed in a black sport coat and skirt. Her red hair framed her head like a helmet. She stood at attention, holding a clipboard in front of her like a shield.

As I joined others filing off the bus, I could see her talking to couples as her assistant handed them keys. She looked as polished as a news anchor in the midst of a disaster scene. When I gave her my name, she said in a voice that sounded aristocratic to my American ears, "Bishop and Mrs. Taylor, you are staying in Tyler Court. I am pleased to say it will be very convenient for you as it is next to the program tent."

I felt blessed. How considerate of the English.

Jo and I trudged across the campus with our four suitcases. We found Tyler Court, but we couldn't find our rooms. The building had four halls spiking out from a courtyard in the middle. It looked like a failed 1960s architectural experiment—concrete and glass. We lugged our suitcases hall by hall. No B5 and B6.

I was sweating and lightheaded. Awake for twenty-two hours, I could no longer think. Standing in the courtyard I saw a man wearing a uniform walking through one of the halls. "Stay here," I barked at Jo.

I ran and reached him just as he was about to enter the elevator. I grabbed his arm and tugged him, turning him to face me. "B5. B6. Where?"

He pulled back and stretched as if to stiff-arm me. Then he saw my shirt and gold cross. We stared at each other. He looked at his watch, took a deep breath and exhaled. A forced smile came on his face. "Of course. Those are in the basement. Hard to find."

He led us down into the building's bowels. Our rooms were on a light-brown tiled hall with five others. One toilet. One shower. Jo and I had separate rooms next to each other. Single bed. One window. Small desk facing a concrete wall.

I put my luggage in the corner. When I went into Jo's room I found her sitting on her narrow mattress with her hands over her face. She sobbed. I knelt in front of her and pulled her hands into mine.

"I can't do this," she said. "We have to live in some cave. One closet bathroom. Six other strangers. Not together."

"It will be…" But what would it be? "We'll make it through," was the best I could do.

The red-faced clock read 4:15 a.m. as I turned off the light. I tapped on the wall as a goodnight but no tap back.

I don't know if the banging of pots and pans or the smell of sausage woke me. The clock read 6:15. Coffee was too important to trust to the English. I had brought my Melita cone and filters and four pounds of Starbucks. Three cups of coffee, one quick shower (remembering I was one of seven), and one CLIF bar, were my preparations to meet the Anglican Communion. I let Jo sleep and walked into the dark English morning.

* * *

"As bishops we are deeply unreliable allies."

The Archbishop of Canterbury kept speaking, but I stopped listening. How can you be an ally if you are unreliable?

This was our second day. I was dazzled. The bishops were on retreat in the Canterbury Cathedral. The archbishop gave a lecture in the morning followed by a period of prayer and reflection, which almost everyone interpreted as sightseeing in the Cathedral. I sat wedged in a pew with the other six hundred purple-shirted bishops, but my mind wasn't completely there. Before I left the Diocese of Western North Carolina, I had met with the Gay/Lesbian Committee.

"You'll be tempted to make peace on our backs, Porter. Don't." Their voices overlaid the archbishop's. I sat staring at his straggly gray hair and his eyebrows so long they fanned across his forehead. He stood tall in his black cassock. His deep baritone voice bounced off the walls. In some sense I felt a kinship with him. Smart, very spiritual, an accomplished writer and poet. A man who could talk about Julian of Norwich or George Herbert or the history of the episcopy from the Second Century forward.

Yet he did not seem to have much political savvy. More than once in his tenure, he had clearly been outmaneuvered and outmatched. When the Diocese of Durham wanted to call a celibate gay priest as their bishop, first he said, "Yes," but then when the church and the crown leaned on him, he said, "No." Most recently when the Africans threatened not to come to Lambeth if he invited Gene Robinson (the Episcopal bishop who was in a partnered relationship), he caved and refused to invite him because of the uproar. Of course, the same African bishops didn't come anyway, so the archbishop got the worst of both worlds.

Even with those reservations, I was looking for him to be a mentor—a kind of Merlin or Gandalf. I came in seeing no way out of the conflict between the progressive West and the very conservative African bishops. I hoped that his brain power would be enough. After all, on his sabbatical, he wrote a book on Dostoevsky in his spare time. I wanted to see how someone who was aesthetic and aloof could negotiate a crisis or at least get in the trenches. Maybe I could follow.

"I have been taken hold by Christ. I belong to Christ. And that be-longing is something deeper and more significant than any other kind of belonging," he said.

I had to grip the seat underneath me to calm down. "You've missed the whole point," I wanted to scream. "Belonging to Christ doesn't lift you above belonging to others; it pushes you further into it. You become everyone's ally."

My agitation wasn't primarily over the Anglican Communion. There was all kind of talk about it splitting. After all, most of the African bishops refused to attend. However, if the Communion was real, it would survive the recent hubbub. If not, was it worth my being bothered?

My distress was inner instead of outer. I felt isolated as the bishop and was looking for a different model. The last thing I wanted to hear was that allies are unreliable because being a bishop had put me into a bubble.

Laypeople and priests treated me with respect and deference, but they didn't open their hearts or lives to me. When I walked into a room, usually people got quiet. I couldn't remember the last time I went to the hospital to pray with the sick, or the funeral home to console the grieving. A priest came to see me to confess some transgression, and I had to tell her to find someone else because as the bishop I might have to discipline her. I was looking for reliable allies.

My bishop world focused on rules and structures and problems. I was the policeman, the judge, and the garbage man. One Wednesday night I stood in front of a church full of people who were angry because their priest tried to seduce the youth worker. "There's really only so much I can say about this because of the possibility of litigation," I heard myself say though I knew it sounded as if I were in the Watergate hearings.

When the archbishop said that Christ was his only friend, my thought was, *That's me. But I need more than one reliable ally. I need a community of allies I can rely on and who can rely on me.*

I feared I would be a man in a uniform, superficially connected to everyone but close to no one. I had spent four years trying to be an ally to the faithful in the diocese yet wondered if I had lost myself in the process. I wondered if I would have been better off not trying to be an ally to people who sing Praise Music and wave their hands but don't give to help the hungry, or the clergy who always want to play King of the Mountain by reminding me of my shortcomings.

I was afraid of losing myself in the bishop's role. I feared constantly running for approval in a way that I would lose my soul and sense of direction. I was terrified of being surrounded by unreliable allies and becoming an unreliable ally because I couldn't take the heat.

Had I gotten my calling upside down?

Since the archbishop is the smartest person in the Anglican Communion, I thought he could give me a direction, but maybe he was as lost as I was.

While the archbishop spoke, the sea of purple shirts looked like a communion. But when he stopped speaking, I heard Spanish and French and African dialects and Australian twangs and Irish brogues. It was vegetable soup. Although we looked uniform, I wondered how we'd be allies when we couldn't even understand one another.

\* \* \*

Jo and I met outside the University cafeteria for lunch the first day after the bishops' retreat.

"How were the spouses?" I asked.

"Most of them testified that Jesus was their personal Lord and Savior."

I looked over her head wondering which way this conversation would go. "What did you say?"

"Nothing. Tell me, what are we doing here? One of the African women said she was glad she was wife number one because number two had to do more housework. Why are they angry at us for ordaining Gene Robinson if some are polygamous? I feel as if I'm in a time warp."

The cafeteria was jammed. The cacophony of different languages bounced off the red tiled walls. Jo and I picked up our trays and moved to get in line as if we were back in grade school.

Suddenly Jo pushed into me, making me stumble forward. When I turned around, I saw her facing off with a large Black woman with a green turban on her head who was jabbing her tray at Jo. The woman's eyes were wide, and her head bobbed up and down in rhythm with her non-English denunciations. She reminded me of a street preacher telling shoppers they were going to hell.

"What's going on?" I asked in my bishop's voice.

Jo's face was bright red and taut. Her lips quivered. "This woman hit me in the back with her tray. She must think I broke in line."

"Screw this," I said. We left our empty trays on the serving line in front of the ranting woman and walked into the cloudy English day.

"Here's the thing," I said. "Not many of these people like The Episcopal Church. One, we ordained Gene Robinson. Two, George Bush is the US president. And three, America has pushed the world around for a long time. It's not personal."

"When they hit you in the back, it's personal."

We walked across the quadrangle and found a small café off campus. The food was not great—soup and a green lump that was called a salad—but for a moment we had a separate peace.

Over a cup of tepid coffee, I said, "So back to the Bible study. What did you say to all that?"

"I said I thought the Bible had something to do with feeding the hungry and clothing the naked and housing the homeless. I said it wasn't just about personal salvation."

"And?"

"And one woman from Tanzania said Americans should be the last people to talk about helping the disadvantaged since they robbed other nations to get where they are."

We sat looking out the café window—shoppers, businesspeople, a few students. None cared about us or the Lambeth Conference. Looking at them made part of me yearn to be walking down my hometown street, deciding whether to go to the bookstore or to get a latte at the coffee shop.

But then I remembered. Was I becoming an "unreliable ally"? Did it take a shove in my wife's back to say "screw it" to the Anglican Communion? What was I willing to bear for some deeper sense of church?

* * *

The agenda listed a topic for the bishops to focus on each day: Anglican Identity, Evangelism, Social Justice, Environmental Concerns, Ecumenism, Scripture, and Human Sexuality. We all knew that we were there to talk about Gene Robinson.

In 2003, The Episcopal Church ordained the first person in a same-sex partnered relationship to become a bishop. There was a tremor across the American Church but an earthquake across the Anglican Communion. Whole countries threatened to leave and start a theologically pure Communion. A bishop from Africa created a pure version of Lambeth in Africa for the theologically correct bishops a month earlier. They told the archbishop to bring them the head of The Episcopal Church or at least to put us in time out forever.

In designing Lambeth, the Archbishop of Canterbury either had a stroke of genius or plunged into denial. He decided there would be no resolutions and no votes—only conversation. He borrowed a South African term "Indaba" to describe our sessions. We were to engage one another in deep listening and simply record what was said. It reminded me of the strategy suggested to Jo and me by a marriage counselor: "There's no right or wrong here," she said. "Just the true data we can unearth."

To my shock, it mainly worked. We were assigned randomly to groups of forty. When we gathered in these groups, we began by talking in clumps of six and then twelve and then twenty-four until we gathered as a whole. Everyone didn't play nice, but most did. In one of our smaller clusters, a bishop from Nigeria called me a heretic because we Americans allowed divorced men and women to remarry. "Jesus said, 'anyone who divorces his wife causes her to commit adultery; and whoever marries a divorced woman commits adultery,' " he quoted and then added, "Either you believe in the Word of God, or you don't."

He looked at me not in anger but with a look of almost pity on his face. Just as I was about to offer a rejoinder, a proper English voice said, "Yes, yes.

But of course, you Africans can say that because you haven't been exposed to the historical critical method. No reputable scholar would claim this teaching is literally binding." The speaker held his eyebrows up and wore a purple skull cap. Our group stared at the floor in embarrassment.

Next to the Nigerian bishop sat a short bishop from Kenya. He had a round face and short, cropped hair. A large silver cross hung on his chest. I knew him from our small Bible study group that met early each morning.

He said in a soft voice, "Yes brother, it may be that those of us from Africa are uneducated bishops. We do not have universities like your Cambridge. However, instead of studying the historical critical method, your brother bishop here walks for eight days to visit his parishes. And brother, he now has two more daughters in his house because their parents have died of AIDS. So maybe he and I are ignorant bishops, but our people don't mind so long as we are with them."

"Well, yes. Of course, we all strive to be pastors," the English bishop stammered.

"Maybe I shouldn't be looking at the Archbishop of Canterbury," I thought as I nodded toward the Kenyan bishop. "Maybe I should look at you."

\* \* \*

The archbishop tried to banish unpleasantness, but it was a fool's errand. In the five years since The Episcopal Church's ordination of a gay man as a bishop in 2003 several commissions had been formed to come up with a way to hold the Communion together. On the afternoon of the third day, The Windsor Group held a hearing for bishops to hear their report about The Episcopal Church and the aftermath of 2003. I could not agree with the report because it said that for the sake of unity, no church in the Communion should do anything that would upset other churches. It sounded like my mother saying at Sunday dinner, "Let's don't talk about anything unpleasant at the table." Of course, it felt to us Americans like a one-way street. We needed to muzzle gays and lesbians, but what about polygamy in Africa or sexism in England? How about the Brits not ordaining women as bishops? Weren't these items upsetting? The format was open mic.

The first speaker was the bishop of Egypt. Short, balding with a bad combover, and pinched features, he spoke with a high-pitched, reedy voice. "Sin is sin. The American Church is now apostate. They must repent by removing this homosexual from our church or they must be removed. There is no compromise with sin."

Unfortunately, it was action—reaction. Three American bishops spoke, which only threw fuel on the fire. In a no-win game, it is best not to play. I wondered if I had become the archbishop. *Have my astute perceptions become my excuse to sit on the sidelines?*

A retired bishop from Canada gave what he called a history lesson, but it was like listening to Rush Limbaugh talk about the Democratic Party. He gave a list of the heresies committed by the American Church.

When I saw one of our louder American bishops go to the mic, I left the room. I had heard his speech too many times. I liked to say, "Conversation leads to conversion which opens us to communion," but this was not true on this day.

* * *

On Thursday, day five, we all went to London to meet Queen Elizabeth, or at least to see her. Because Jo was leaving Saturday, we booked a hotel room. I planned to play hooky on Friday. Maybe I could remember *normal*.

I wasn't that thrilled about going to Buckingham Palace. I was too American, too egalitarian, and too fed up with the British pomposity. Jo and I managed to stow our luggage at the hotel and rejoin the bishops at a luncheon with the prime minister. I had read in the *Guardian* that his poll numbers were in the tank. According to the writer, he simply was ineffective. The rumor was that he was being pressured to call for elections by his own party because they were eager to get in someone who could get something done.

Before lunch, we gathered in a courtyard. The wind whipped his hair across his face, forcing him to hold it down with one hand even as he punctuated his words with his other. I was looking at my watch, eager for lunch.

He gave a knockout speech. "Justice is what all men and women hunger for, and it's the job of government and the call of the church to respond to that hunger."

He had a deep baritone that pushed his words against his listeners. "We cannot stand idle so long as people are hungry, or they lack medicine or food or health care. When one is diminished so are we all."

I wondered if since reelection seemed doubtful, he found his voice. I wondered about the archbishop and me. Were we just too stuck in navigating the political mine fields to speak the truth? If I found my voice, would I find allies? Or if I knew I was done, would I be free to speak?

After lunch we boarded buses for Buckingham Palace. We bishops wore purple cassocks (no skull cap for me). Wives were instructed to wear hats and closed shoes.

Jo spent more time on finding a hat than she did on selecting her wedding dress. She wore an olive linen skirt and pink jacket and a very dapper straw hat. I told her she looked like a twenty-first century Diana Rigg from *The Avengers*, but her expression told me I was off the mark.

In the middle of London, the royal family has a fifteen-acre garden. To get there we had to go through the tightest security I had seen. No phones, no cameras, no briefcases. Metal detectors, scanners, purses checked. We walked through a hallway with ceilings two stories high into a formal garden with a lake shining into the distance. We were no longer in London. No city noises. Trees grew so high the only visible rooftop was the palace.

Tents were set up, but no one ate before the queen. Jo and I walked through the gardens. Not lavish or opulent, but exquisite. Everything quietly correct. Flowers bordering the paths and the lake. Old oaks and bending willows. The wind made the sun sparkle on the water. I thought, even a queen needs a garden—a place to remember her Christian name.

As we returned to the palace, we could see two lines forming along the pathway. I had been lukewarm about all this. But as Jo and I weaseled our way to the front, I felt like those teenagers at JFK waiting for the Beatles to arrive in 1964. We faced the doors to the Royal Apartments, which were up a steep flight of outdoor steps.

The first person to emerge was the queen's lady-in-waiting. She wore a stylish gray jacket and skirt with a hat that looked like she was the fourth Musketeer. Her blonde hair hung around her shoulders. As she walked from the steps to the crowd, she extended her hand to the archbishop. They spoke and chuckled together.

Next came the Palace Guards—red coats with "ER" embroidered on their pockets and black hats. They marched out in two columns and came to stand in front of our lines. Hands on hips, elbows preventing anyone from royal territory.

Finally, she came out. Kelly green suit and hat. At eighty-four she walked down the steps without cane or assistance. After she greeted the archbishop, he bowed to her and she nodded to him. No one shakes the queen's hand. He led her down the two rows to meet selected bishops. Rowan's assistants asked the bishop and spouse to step out into the path and wait for the royal presence.

I was now a total groupie. I stood on my toes and inwardly screamed, *Look at me. See how gorgeous my wife is with her new hat.*

Prince Philip walked over to us and said to me, "And where is your home?"

"North Carolina, in the US," I replied.

When he smiled, I saw his teeth were crooked and yellow, but his smile was broad and genuine. "You in the colony do come tall, don't you?"

As I was about to answer, one of the spouses stuck out her hand beneath the guard's arms and blurted, "I am overjoyed to meet you, Your Majesty."

The prince didn't look at her but turned his face and walked on.

Finally, the queen and the royal party invited the Primates (heads of national churches) into her tent for tea. The rest of us went to a separate tent for tea, scones, pastries, and small triangle sandwiches. I took my cup and stood so I could watch the other tent. What I did not see was Rowan Williams talk to Bishop Katharine, the head of the American Church and only female Primate, in the tent. The archbishop was inviting bishops to speak with Her Majesty. But I didn't see him invite her. I wondered if this was what unreliable meant.

The scones tasted stale, and the sandwiches were soggy.

Then we were done. Jo and I walked to our hotel, glad to have a respite from the Communion. That afternoon we went to The Courtauld Gallery, tucked away in a quadrangle of government buildings. Jo had read that it contained Impressionist paintings as well as Renaissance and Medieval religious art.

We walked into a windowless floor with small rooms where only the paintings were illuminated. I didn't get past the first room. I stopped in front of a painting of the crucifixion, by Botticelli, *The Trinity with Saints*. The crucified Christ is in the middle between John the Baptist and Mary Magdalene. I didn't look at the saints or Jesus. I looked at the bottom left corner where two miniature figures appeared to be walking off the canvas.

The angel is in a muted red robe walking upright and bending his head to the other figure, perhaps in instruction. The other person is dressed in black and is obscured by the angel except for his face which is upturned in rapt attention, and in his right hand he holds something.

The description beside the painting informed me that the figures were the angels Raphael and Tobias, from the apocryphal book of the Bible, Tobit. Tobit tells a convoluted story about an old blind father and his city Nineveh being on the brink of destruction by God. Therefore, Tobias had to leave home to find a boon. He caught a fish that gave sight to his father (by his concocting a disgusting fish broth), helped Tobias find his true love (he had to burn the fish liver and heart to drive away anti-marriage demons), and enabled them to escape Nineveh before it was destroyed.

I stared at the crucifixion and at Tobias and the angel in the corner. Maybe I had gotten my calling upside down. Maybe I wasn't called just to be a figurehead for everyone's projections. Maybe I couldn't be the Queen who found herself in her office. Even if I could get fifteen acres of garden inside the city, would it be space enough to grow? I knew I couldn't be Rowan Williams who seemed to have lost himself in the trappings of his office.

Instead, maybe like Tobias, my calling was to go fishing beyond the prescribed borders. As I stared at the painting, I realized that I couldn't fix the Anglican Communion or The Episcopal Church or anything really. But if I could find Raphael, maybe he would lead me somewhere that might not make sense to anyone, but that might change everything.

I wasn't sure what that meant, but I knew it meant movement and connection and more than I could grasp in that moment. I knew I had to get beyond the crucifix and follow some book that wasn't even in most people's Bibles. I needed to get beyond the fence I was penned in.

* * *

The last day I was already mentally on the airplane. I wanted to see my children, sleep in my bed, and focus on what mattered to people whose names I knew. I expected an English version of a warm fuzzy sendoff.

After the Eucharist, the archbishop introduced the President of Princeton Seminary, a Presbyterian, a Scotsman who told us not to rock the ecumenical boat. Then he called on the Bishop of the English branch of the Greek Orthodox Church who told us that since homosexuality was a sin in the third century, it was still a sin.

Neither made me feel good about what might come.

The archbishop stood behind the pulpit and handed out the expected platitudes. We clapped for the staff.

Then he said, "There is only one way forward. We must have a Covenant that holds us mutually accountable for our actions. If one part of the Communion acts in a way that others find unbiblical or threatens the bonds of mutual affection, then they must stop their behavior or step outside the Communion." I knew that "one part" meant the American part.

Bait and switch I thought. He said "no votes; no resolutions" because his was the only vote that counts, and he had written his own resolution. He had gone beyond unreliable. He was no longer an ally.

I didn't hear the rest. It was all about the process and procedures, who would meet when and so forth, but I had heard enough. It was wheels within the wheels. It was all about abstract principles and structures far away from the warp and woof of real life. I needed to be out.

* * *

On the plane home I sat next to a woman from Philadelphia returning from a walking tour of Scotland. She was in her fifties, a therapist who proclaimed to be unchurched. She was affable with no visible sharp edges.

She asked me about the conference and the queen and how the church worked. Finally, she said, "What was the best part?"

"For me, the stories were the best. I like the times between the meetings."

"I'm glad to hear that," she said, "because from the papers it sounded like it wasn't much fun. You church people love to argue about sex, don't you?"

"No, it's not my love." After a pause, I said, "I'm really not clear about what my love is right now, to tell you the truth, but I am clearer about finding it."

We sat in silence for a while. I started reading the only book I recognized in the airport shop—*Plain Truth*, a Jodi Picoult mystery about an Amish family.

The woman touched my arm. "When you get home," she said, "maybe if you ask your people for their stories, those stories will lead you to what you love. Just an idea."

As we flew into the dark western sky, I thought about her words all the way home.

# 10

## Lonely at the Top

There is no thing outside ourselves, no circumstance, no condition, no vicissitude, that can ultimately separate us from the love of God and the love of one another. And we pour out our gratitude to God that this is so.

—HOWARD THURMAN, *THE INWARD JOURNEY*

"BISHOP, THERE'S A CRISIS of confidence in the diocese."

I looked across the conference table in my office at the short overweight priest. He leaned forward in his chair, the table hiding his bulge, and brushed back his brown hair. His silver Celtic cross shone against his black clergy shirt and dark gray suit.

"I assume you mean there's a lack of confidence in me."

I tried to say this in a matter-of-fact tone. He and I needed to stay away from each other. I found him superficial, opinionated, and egotistical. He found me ineffective, detached, and cerebral.

In my office that day, the priest placed his hands on his chest and proclaimed, "The priests don't trust you. They think you'd throw them under the bus if you got the chance." He paused, but I only stared at him. He had said this before. "Bishop, here's a list of complaints."

I crossed my arms and legs. I felt myself pushing back in the chair and tightening my stomach to take the blows. I wore my black suit as a kind of armor, but I realized it was too thin. I took my heavy gold cross out of my left shirt pocket and placed it in the center of my purple shirt. I hoped the amethyst in its middle would be my talisman for what was to come.

He cleared his throat, held up the typed page, and read the list in a formal voice like a foreman for a jury.

"You create committees and then do what you want. The Clergy want you as a pastor, but you are never around. All you talk about is money . . . "

And the list went on and on. My favorite was, "You quote from obscure German poets in your sermons." When he finished, he lifted his gaze and looked directly at me as if to say, "So there."

Some of these were accurate. Some were helpful, but the underlying message was, "From now on, you are the identified patient. Whatever is wrong with anything is your fault."

In 2009 my heart was more open because I hadn't been scarred enough to become highly defensive. I had only been the bishop for five years. On a retreat earlier that year I was praying alone in the monastery chapel—staring at the cross—when I remembered some words from my consecration: "May you [the new bishop] present before God a pure, gentle, and holy life." For the past five years I thought if I stayed centered in prayer each day and didn't get jaded by the business of the diocese, I could lead by an example of holiness. If I tried to listen and honestly respond, if I tried to let the Spirit do what she wills, if I assumed the best in people, then others would respond in kind. I don't mean my behavior was close to being pure or gentle or holy, but those were my intentions.

Sitting across from this priest, I felt like a fool. I had been naïve about the church and being bishop. Maybe instead of spending my time praying, I should have been talking to a political consultant.

During his litany of complaints my face flushed, and my pulse quickened. I grabbed the sides of the table in an effort to calm down. How had I come to this? Five years before I had been happy in my small parish in the woods of Athens, Georgia. I wasn't making headlines, but the work was grounded in the everyday lives of people—comforting the sick, burying the dead, marrying young couples, teaching people about the mysteries of the faith. Most of all, I felt more aligned with a sense of mission and purpose and less an object for people's projections. If people didn't like their priest, they could go to the other Episcopal Church across town or not go to church. But as the bishop, we were stuck with each other.

"Let me ask you some questions." My voice was too loud, so I coughed and tried again in a more controlled tone.

"How would you suggest I pastor to seventy priests and carry out the other functions of a bishop?"

"Can you think of a way to fund our budget without talking about money?

It was a fool's errand. I felt as if I had become Richard Nixon, and it didn't matter if I started the Peace Corps, I would always be Tricky Dick for this priest and his gang. The irony was that I was a good pastor one on one, but I usually had those exchanges about radioactive subjects, and, therefore, I couldn't talk about them publicly.

I wanted to say, "What about the priest who got so depressed she couldn't come out of her house, and couldn't cook her children's meals? What about the hours I spent with her? What about the disability I got for her?"

I wanted to say, "What about the priest who came into my office and said, 'I have something to tell you. I am gay and I don't know how to tell my wife.' What about my role in helping them part?"

I wanted to say, "What about the rector of a parish who told me she no longer believed in God and asked, 'What am I supposed to say on Sunday, Bishop?' What about my counseling her?"

I wanted to say more, but I couldn't say anything. Faithful men and women asked me to hold these things in my heart. They weren't resume items I could point to as proof of my being pastoral.

Then there was my temperament. It's true I was terrible at cocktail parties. I didn't drink. I didn't care about sports. I didn't know any jokes. I was aloof and bookish and private. I made a terrible candidate for anything—especially "Most Popular Bishop."

I spoke in generalities with this priest, but I was getting nowhere. I didn't even sound convincing to myself. While I talked, he looked over my head at the print of Botticelli's *Lamentation over the Dead Christ* hanging on my wall. When I was finished, he parried my questions and then said, "You are deflecting the main point, Bishop. This isn't about data. It's about you."

\* \* \*

I went to see my spiritual director, a wise retired pastor. I told him about the complaints and how defensive and hurt I felt. He was a wise retired progressive Baptist pastor. He smiled and told me, "If you close off your heart, everyone loses." We sat in his basement study, the walls lined with bookshelves and the tables littered with manuscripts. My director was in his mid-seventies and looked like Jason Robards: tall, silver haired, and crevasses lining his face. He had a deep laugh and would sometimes tap his worn Bible lying in his lap with his forefinger as he thought.

"I am tired of getting hammered," I said, "and I am tired of everything being my fault."

"For better or worse, you are the compost for the diocese," he replied. "And," he added, "compost takes time to make good soil and it generates some heat."

"You may be right, but you forgot: sometimes compost smells."

He told me to meet with clergy and to stay centered and open.

Then he added, "Porter, some months ago you told me about a prayer you've been using. Remember?"

I only nodded because I knew what was coming.

"Here's the key line for you, and it's the one for you to pray at this Clergy Day," he said as he opened his black leather-bound journal, turned the pages and read: "Welcome, welcome, welcome. I welcome everything that comes to me today, because I know it's for my healing."

"I know that," I blurted. He was quoting from "The Welcoming Prayer" by Father Thomas Keating.[1] To stay centered, I had taped this on my desk so I would read it before every meeting. I paused and stared at him. "Well, I am trying to know that, and I am hoping to believe it."

* * *

The Clergy Day was billed as a "conversation," but I feared it would be all one way. It was held at the Diocesan Conference Center, nestled next to the Pisgah National Forest. It was a clear October day. In the middle of the Center was a pristine lake. Its surface reflected the red and yellow leaves.

Our meeting was in the dining hall which overlooked the lake and a mountain ridge. I asked the staff to put the chairs in a large circle against the walls. Looking out the window, I could see the ripples the wind stirred up on the lake and the dappled leaves spinning between tree and water. I stood in the far corner of the room as the clergy trooped in from lunch. There were around fifty priests and deacons, all dressed informally—jeans, sweatshirts, baseball caps. Like them, no collar for me. I saw the priest who had come to my office. He sat in the back, as far from me as he could get. He was with a group, and I tried not to think of conspiracies.

There was little conversation. People talked the way they do before funerals. My director and I had structured the afternoon into three sessions: "What we like," "What we can do better," "Where we want to go." Twenty minutes each. No speeches. No back and forth. Just listing the responses.

---

1. Keating, "Welcoming Prayer," lines 1–2.

"Get it all in front of you," my director had said. "What you can see is better than what you fear." But was it? "Welcome, welcome, welcome?"

I could feel my neck muscles tighten and I realized my breaths were getting shorter and shorter. I sensed someone standing next to me. A priest I admired was shoulder to shoulder with me, looking at the gathering crowd.

"Hey. Must be lonely at the top, huh?"

"Thank you for your support. I mean it," I said.

"Don't worry. You still got Jesus."

I looked at him to see how to take this and saw that he was smiling and gently nodding his head. He leaned over, put his hand on my shoulder, and softly said, "It'll be fine. You're our bishop whatever gets said."

I began with prayer: "Give us grace seriously to lay to heart the great dangers we are in by our unhappy divisions." Then the three sessions with breaks in between. Whenever anyone spoke, I made myself walk toward them until I was six feet away. I fixed my gaze on them so they would know I wasn't afraid of their comments. I would nod my head, and at the end of their comments, say their name and thank them for their input. I repeated what they said so that the priest recording everything on newsprint could write it down. I was trying to give the appearance of "Welcome, welcome, welcome."

But I wasn't welcoming any of this. I was hurt. I was wounded. I felt alone and forsaken. Throughout the session I was thinking, "Why in the world have I come to this place with these people?"

I have a copy of every comment spoken in that hour. When I read the comments later, I realized they were not personal or even highly negative. The clergy mainly said they wanted to see me more and hear me preach more and get me freed up from fundraising so I could do more of what I love.

Looking back, I realized there was a gap between the record and my experience. Despite what the newsprint said, what I heard was:

"You don't know us, and you don't care about us."

"We don't trust you, and we don't respect you."

I thought about this gap and hated my conclusions. As much as I yearned for affirmation, part of me was incapable of believing it. Instead, my interior editor clutched the one critical voice in a chorus of accolades. It seemed to me that people like the complaining priest were external affirmations of a ledger lodged in my heart, listing my essential unworthiness.

Bishops are screens for everyone's projections. Three days after my consecration I went to a meeting of all the bishops in The Episcopal Church. When I met the Presiding Bishop, my first day there, he leaned over and said, "This job is different from anything else. Remember one thing: you will get more praise and more blame than you deserve. Don't trust either one." I did more than trust the negative half. I embraced it because it echoed some secret about my flawed self that I could neither name nor relinquish. In that long list of comments written on the newsprint, the ones I wrote on my heart were about my shortcomings because deep inside I knew they were true.

\* \* \*

When my feet touched the carpet, the room began to spin. Not a twirl, but the inside of a tornado. My stomach lurched and I put my hand over my mouth to stifle the vomit. I began to sweat. I eased myself back into the bed and lay completely still.

"Jo." When she didn't answer, I pushed her with my left hand. "Jo. I can't get up. My head is spinning so fast I almost threw up."

"It's vertigo. Stay still." Always the nurse.

"I can't stay still. I have to pee. Please help me up."

I felt ninety years old. I put one arm around Jo and stuck my right arm out like one of The Great Wallendas seeking balance.

Back in bed, she said, "Let me read up on this. Just lie there."

"I can't just lie here. I have to ordain a young man in four hours."

It was May 30, 2009. The Diocese had sent out invitations for the ordination to the priesthood months ago. Only bishops could ordain priests, and I was the only bishop within four hours. I wasn't indispensable for many things, but this was one. They didn't need me to preach or pray or even preside, but they needed my hands on his head.

Jo returned. "Well, he can just get ordained without you. I can't find anything helpful."

"No. Actually he can't. There's no other bishop here."

She gave me her look—eyebrows knitted, head tilted forward, lips pursed. "That's ridiculous," she said. "Who are you—Superman? Of course, someone else can ordain him. Call the retired bishop; call Upper South Carolina. Or just tell him to wait a week. You can't even walk to the bathroom much less down the church aisle."

But I knew the retired bishop was out of town, and I knew the candidate's extended family was coming from all over the Southeast, as well as members from his parish and his fellow seminarians. I didn't want to put a note on the Cathedral door saying, "Come back next week, the bishop can't make it."

I stayed in bed for an hour while Jo made her calls. None of our friends had experienced vertigo. Somehow, I got back to the bathroom. If I focused on one spot, my balance was a little better. I was afraid to get in the shower, but I shaved, and despite Jo's barrage of reasons not to go, she helped me get dressed.

I couldn't stand for a long time, but I thought I could tolerate sitting. I went downstairs—purple shirt, black suit, gold cross, ready to go.

Jo made pancakes. I sat ramrod straight and kept my eyes on the plate. I stood to put my dishes in the sink.

"You look awful," Jo said.

"I'm fine," I tried to say, but before I got the words out, I vomited across the kitchen just like in *The Exorcist*—a brown stream splattering against the sink. I slumped into the chair and put my head on the kitchen table. I was sweating and heaving.

"Look at yourself. Why do you do this? My God! Projectile vomiting and you think you can go to church? Really?"

I sat for a while on the couch with a cold washcloth on my forehead.

"Call the deacon at the Cathedral," I told Jo. "Ask her to meet me at the car and tell her I cannot stand for any of the service. I will walk in, sit down, and walk out."

Instead of processing in from the back of the church, I walked in from the side, led by the deacon, like King Lear and Cordelia. The deacon was a no-nonsense, solid woman. My right hand was on her left shoulder, and she gripped my left hand in hers. "I won't let you fall," she whispered when we were halfway to the chair. "Just hold on." To prevent the spinning, I stared at the stained-glass window in the side transept of Lady Charity shielding two children with her flowing blue robe.

I sat in the Bishop's Chair in the middle of the church and looked straight ahead at the back door. I wondered if the priest who complained in my office was thinking I was so pompous that I now refused to process into the service. I didn't stand for the hymns or the Creed or the Eucharistic Prayer. I sat still.

When the young ordinand came and knelt before me, the archdeacon helped me stand. I reached out my hands and held his head with both of them. As I said the words of ordination, I realized I was gripping his head to keep myself steady.

In the recession, the acolytes and choir flowed around me. I was the boulder in the stream. Everyone was in motion but me. Everyone sang but me. Everyone went over to the Parish Hall for a party but me. I could not join them because my world was spinning. It was all I could do to avoid throwing up in the Cathedral.

When the crowd had gone, the deacon came and led me out. Jo was waiting by the car. She still had the look of "Why do you do these things to yourself?"

I got home, but in the days and months and years following, the spinning never stopped.

* * *

In the fall of 2012, I was at an emotional low. I had been fundraising for two years to eliminate the multimillion-dollar debt that had greeted me upon my arrival as bishop, with little real support. One person was even rude. "Stop asking us for funds to pay off your debts," a letter from the rector stated. I was tired and even though I had been successful in the campaign, I was deflated.

Being the bishop is like being in charge of UNESCO. No one knows what the diocese is, and, therefore, no one knows what your job is. They think it's unconnected to their lives, and they suspect most of the work is meaningless bureaucracy.

On the upcoming Sunday I was to serve at a church about two hours away. The priest there asked if I could come to the eight o'clock service as well as the ten thirty. I figured he wanted all of his people to see me, but I suspected he also didn't want to have to write a sermon for the small crowd at the early service.

"Glad to come," I said, but I wasn't. I'd either have to leave my house at five thirty in the morning or spend Saturday night away. I booked a room at the nearby Hampton Inn knowing I seldom slept well in a strange bed.

I got to the church at seven thirty Sunday morning with a low-level resentment. I felt put upon. There were twenty-five people there. I preached but received no energy from "the frozen chosen" as we call "the eight o'clockers."

After the service, I stood by the door shaking hands as people exited. A short, white-haired woman with a camel overcoat approached me with her hand extended. I had no memory of ever seeing her. When I took her hand, I said, "It's a pleasure to meet you. I'm Porter Taylor."

"I know who you are, and I want to tell you something." Her voice was a deep Charleston drawl. Still holding my hand, she pulled me closer to her until her mouth was inches from my ear. I could smell her hairspray as the stiff strands brushed my cheek.

"You are a wonderful bishop. I think you're the best I've ever known. I hope you know that, and I hope you never forget it."

I did not know why I kept forgetting the many parts I loved about being the bishop. I loved visiting parishes on Sunday. I loved my staff. I loved helping parishes do innovative ministry and I loved working with my fellow bishops, but I was tired and needed to do something else.

\* \* \*

Every spring the junior high school students from across the Diocese come to Valle Crucis Conference Center near Boone, North Carolina, for Spring Conference. There are talks and hikes and a Saturday night dance. I made an appearance at most of those to show the young people that they mattered.

In March of 2012, I drove to Valle Crucis to have dinner with the junior high youth and stayed afterward to talk. We sat around the fireplace in the Inn. There were about thirty youth, the boys much more awkward and self-conscious than the girls. From my vantage point, it looked like the orthodontists in Western North Carolina were doing a great business. "How about another Emily Dickinson poem, bishop?" one of the boys asked.

In 2011 the junior high held a talent show and the youth worker on my staff told me I had to have an act. I didn't sing. I didn't play any instruments. I didn't want to read a sermon. So, I googled "Dickinson rap" and found a YouTube of two teenagers rapping Dickinson poems. They waved their arms in the air with their index and small fingers extended and yelled "Yo, yo, yo" a lot. I couldn't recognize the music, and I couldn't figure out what tune, if any, they were keeping. They were a long way from my adolescent experience, but their performance was short—less than three minutes. I could do almost anything for three minutes.

The night of the show, I arrived wearing my purple shirt but brought a grocery bag with my rap outfit. As one of the teenagers recited a poem, I went to a back corner of the room and put on my blue hooded Sewanee sweatshirt and let my gold cross dangle in front. The last touch was a pair of sunglasses.

I stood in front of the sea of teenagers and shouted, "When I say Emily, you say Dickinson." We went back and forth three times with me acting like a cheerleader stirring up the crowd. Then the music started and I kind of bobbed around and in my lowest voice intoned Emily Dickinson's "Some keep the Sabbath going to Church." I especially lengthened the last word of "I keep it, staying at Home." I extended my fingers as the YouTube boys did. After my three minutes, I bowed. The kids whooped and hollered. They could relate to a sweat-shirted, sun-glassed man making a fool of himself more than a pious, overeducated, detached sixty-one-year-old bishop talking about the church.

I told the boy by the fire at the Spring Conference: "No, no repeat performances. I am one and done." Looking around the room, I asked, "Why don't you guys tell me what you've been up to this weekend?"

Silence. Finally, I pointed to a girl with long blonde hair, only because she was willing to make eye contact with me. "Tell me about the weekend."

She blushed. "I don't know. We talked about how to help people and we took a hike. I am hoping we can take a field trip to the Mast General Store tomorrow."

"Thanks. Anyone else? Tell what y'all do when you aren't in church."

It was hard sledding. They were embarrassed, and I couldn't get on their wavelength. After a long lull, a girl wearing a green Camp Henry sweatshirt asked me, "Do you love your job?"

I couldn't find the words to respond. I knew I should say, "Absolutely." But I could not do it. I looked at her, and then I looked at my youth worker, and then I looked at the molding above the group's head. The only sound was the crackling of the fire.

"Well," I said as I exhaled. "That's really not the question. It's not about loving your job. It's about being called. We do a lot of things we don't love, right? Do y'all always love to do your homework, or exercise, or your chores?"

They stared stone-faced. "I mean, I love parts of my job, but I am called to do all kinds of things for the church because they need to be done and I serve the church."

No energy back from them. "But," I said raising my voice, "I always love being with you. You're not the future of the church. You're the best of the church right now."

This was better. At least they nodded. One boy said, "Amen to that."

"And, who knows?" I said, "Maybe next time, we'll have another Dickinson poem."

"Which one?" one of the boys yelled.

"Hope is the thing with feathers that perches in the soul," I replied. "Anyone know that one?" No one did.

As I drove home through the night, the question from the girl wearing the green sweatshirt stuck in my head and my heart. I was not a victim. I was appreciated. I felt called. I knew that many people respected and admired me and assumed I was content. I knew I had accomplished some worthy goals, and I regretted very few decisions. I was proud to have ordained and confirmed and blessed. I had been able to travel to extraordinary places including London and India and attended remarkable events like The Lambeth

Conference in England and the Installation of the Presiding Bishop at the National Cathedral. I knew this office was a great privilege. I was only the sixth person to hold it.

But driving down the mountain road in the dark, all I wanted to do was get home and take off my bishop's outfit so I could be more myself than I ever would be in my purple shirt.

Tomorrow I would put my bishop's outfit back on and follow my schedule for the day. I knew I would do my job, but I did not think on that day I would love my job, and because of my makeup and my temperament and my inability to defeat my inner critic, I wondered if I ever could.

# 11

# Katharine Jefferts Schori

The Names of those who in their lives fought for life
Who wore at their hearts the fire's centre
Born of the sun, they traveled a short while towards the sun
And left the vivid air signed with their honor.

—STEPHEN SPENDER, *THE TRULY GREAT*

On SUNDAY, JUNE 18, 2006 at 10:45 a.m. I sat in one of the hard straight back wooden pews of Trinity Episcopal Church in Columbus, Ohio with 188 other bishops. The church had a pleasing aesthetic: high cream-colored arches that reached to a Madonna blue ceiling, red and blue stained-glass windows, and long choir stalls to separate the congregation from the high altar. A big downtown church.

All the bishops wore purple shirts and suits because this was our Episcopal version of a conclave. We were gathered to elect the next head of our church, the 26th Presiding Bishop.

I was jumping out of my skin. I had only been a bishop for eighteen months and was still starstruck. I never thought I would meet the Presiding Bishop, much less have a vote in determining who the successor would be. I sat next to my best friend, Nedi, an assistant bishop. She was one of the twelve female bishops in this sea of men. We had gone together through "Baby Bishop School." I liked her playfulness, and I supposed she appreciated my Soren Kierkegaard demeanor. She laughed loudly and talked a lot and used big gestures and was a life force. Most of all, she wasn't me, and she wasn't the church of stiff white men.

I tugged the sleeve of her black suit jacket. "What are we waiting for?" I said in a stage whisper, "Let's do this."

"Porter," she said, "We're Episcopalians. We have to wallow in pomp and pretentiousness for a while. All the candidates need a last minute to preen."

Since nothing was happening, I stood and looked around. I saw a bishop in the back sitting in a motorized wheelchair in the aisle. He was bigger than Jabba the Hutt. Near him were two white-haired bishops with wrinkled faces, wearing faded purple shirts and seersucker suits. Bending down to Nedi's ear, I asked, "Who are those people? I've never seen them."

"Everyone wants to put their stamp on the future of the church," she said as she stood up to see. "Remember retired bishops get to vote too. They are from very conservative dioceses. Need I say more?"

"So, they're here to do mischief?"

"Wait and see."

Finally, a tall priest in a black clerical shirt and dark suit came to the portable podium in the middle of the aisle and got us quiet by intoning "The Lord be with you."

We said, "And also with you," and he prayed and began to talk.

"I am the rector of Trinity Church. Welcome to our parish and the Diocese of Southern Ohio. As part of our welcome, I'd like to tell you about the history of this parish."

"Crap," I whispered to her. "Can't we just get on with the vote?"

Cocking her head, she gave me the look a mother gives a teenager and shook her head in disapproval, her turquoise blue earrings waving back and forth.

The rector went on with his infomercial about the parish. Just when I thought he was done, he said, "As a memento of this historic occasion, I'd like to give you a commemorative book marking our 200th anniversary."

Men in blazers and women in fashionable dresses appeared in the aisles, handing out books the size of a road atlas. I thought, "One more thing for my suitcase." However, since I am from the South, I said, "Thank you so much." The book had a black-and-white photo of a nineteenth-century Sunday school class on the church steps. Above it were the words "Be It Remembered." I stuffed it into my tote bag and drummed my fingers on the pew in front of me.

Every nine years, one of the active bishops in The Episcopal Church is elected to be the head of the denomination. It doesn't take as long as running for President of the United States, and it costs the candidates almost no money, but the process is political in a tasteful, repressed, Episcopal way. A designated committee decides on a slate from the current bishops—which in many ways is pointless because those not selected can get on the ballot by petition.

The term of Frank Griswold, the 25th Presiding Bishop, expired in 2006. A nominating committee had worked hard to select four bishops as candidates: Neil Alexander from Atlanta, Ted Gulick from Kentucky, Henry Parsley from Alabama, and Katharine Jefferts Schori from Nevada. Three white Southern males against one Western woman. However, the vision of being head of the church was hard to shake. Three candidates that didn't make the final cut were added by petition: Francisco Duque-Gomez from Columbia, South America; Charles Jenkins from Louisiana; and Stacy Sauls from Lexington, Kentucky. Now six white Southern males, one Latino, against one Western woman.

The Convention had already been going on for five days before election day. While we had been doing our usual business of telling the world how to behave—whether the wall should come down in Jerusalem or whether guns were a good idea anywhere—the nominated bishops were circulating all week in the Convention, some grabbing arms and making jokes like Lyndon Johnson.

The early betting was on Henry Parsley from Alabama or Neil Alexander from Atlanta. I liked Henry. Like me, he had studied literature in college, although mainly Southern literature. He gave seminars on Flannery O'Connor and Walker Percy.

Earlier in our March bishops' meeting in Texas, we talked about what the African Anglican bishops thought about our church's ordaining Gene Robinson in 2003, the only openly gay bishop in The Episcopal Church or any church having our common origins from the Church of England, which is what being Anglican is about. Of course, the real topic was not what to say to the churches across the seas. We were sizing up the slate of nominees and they cooperated by getting to the microphone often.

Henry Parsley had polio as a child, which surprised me because we're the same age. I associated polio with people living before 1950. He wore a metal brace extending from his foot to his middle thigh. In our debate, he slowly walked to the microphone and began to talk in a mellow drawl.

He was articulate and informed. I had only been a bishop for eighteen months, but already I wanted to find consensus even for the most contentious issues. In my heart I knew that no leader could make that happen. I discovered that in the end it's not about opinions but about actions over the long haul.

Soon after my election as bishop, one of the influential priests in the diocese asked me, "When are you going to ordain our transitional deacon to the priesthood?" The priest was ten years younger than me and quite handsome. He looked like he belonged on the cover of *Vanity Fair*. "Porter, she's a candidate for the priesthood and is in limbo. She'll be the first priest in our diocese in a partnered relationship. But you'll have to decide yes or no."

"Right. If she finds a job, I'll ordain her. Just like everyone else." But the truth was, I wondered how that would go down in this diocese.

My first few months, I went around the diocese meeting people. I talked to my conservative parishes about finding a middle way and making sure everyone was at the table, and I believed what I was saying at the time.

However, I discovered that honeymoon seasons end, and then you must do one thing and not another. So, one summer evening, I stood beside the transitional deacon at Holy Cross Church in Valle Crucis, North Carolina, and said to the congregation, "She has studied, and trained, and is called to be a priest. I am proud to ordain her because she will do great things for the church we all love." She then knelt before me, and I put my hands on her head.

I received some letters. Some people quit the church. But that was offset by the comfort of thinking I had done the right thing.

Which of these nominees would stand beside that transitional deacon?

Neil Alexander was a real scholar, a former seminary professor, smooth with people, funny, a die-hard Yankees fan. He had rounded shoulders reminiscent of Churchill and a wonderful laugh that bordered on a cackle. Neil had all the tools for the job. He was my bishop when I was in Athens, Georgia, and had always been supportive of me. Plus, I liked him, but because the former Presiding Bishop was so intellectual, I wasn't sure that was the direction we'd take.

I decided to cast my first ballot out of friendship. Ted Gulick was the kindest bishop I knew. He cried more in the pulpit than I did. He had a kind of loud voice. He always squeezed my shoulder when he saw me. He told me that he voted for Gene Robinson in 2003 because "I couldn't love Jesus and not do that." I didn't think Ted could win, but I wanted to support him on this first ballot.

Sitting in Trinity's pew, my friend leaned over and said, "Can you vote for Katharine? You know she's the smartest person in the room."

It was true. In the March 2006 meeting, Katharine Jefferts Schori, Bishop of Nevada, came to the mic and reminded us that she was a former oceanographer and for that reason she thought nature could teach us theology. She went on to describe an event that happens once a year in the Pacific Ocean when whales gather in schools to mate. Apparently, each whale school has a distinct song, and the song they sing helps them find their way. Even more surprising, she said that when they gather once a year, they go away singing a new and different song that will enable them to get back home and remember their connection.

Then she paused and scanned the large ballroom for effect. "I think that's church," she said, and sat down.

The bishops in the audience stared at each other. Who knew quiet Katharine had such imagination and vision?

My first extended conversation with Katharine was in our "Baby Bishop School" in 2005. She was on the faculty and took the lead on "Public Policy."

It was mainly about lobbying your representative or senator and how to deal with the press. She talked about engaging issues on many levels—local, national, and global. Katharine had a melodious voice and appeared somewhat introverted. However, when she looked at you, you were the only person in the room.

At the end of her talk, she leaned on the front table and asked for questions.

"How do we get beyond band-aids to the cause?" one of the bishops asked.

She cocked her head and looked at him. "Do you know what the cause is?" she asked, more curious than confrontational.

"Well, it's racism and sexism and homophobia and American imperialism for a start."

She nodded. "And the root cause. Do you know that?"

I was thinking "sin" or some theological concept, but we all looked at each other and finally at her. She said: "Patriarchy. It's about ending the dominance of privileged white men."

From then on, I listened when she talked because I knew she was not going to be same old same old. But if patriarchy is in charge, could she get elected?

"No, I'm not voting for her this round," I said to Nedi sitting in our hard Christ Church pew. "She's smart; she has vision; she can do the politics; but there's a catch." Nedi raised her eyebrows. "She can't win," I said.

"Wait and see," Nedi replied.

Finally, the assistant bishop from Southern Ohio took the mic. "In a moment we will cast the first ballot. You can only vote for one candidate. You will be given a paper ballot by the tellers."

He coughed loudly into the mic. "By rules of the House of Bishops, the tellers are the five newest bishops: Bishops Taylor, Rivera, Steenson, Mathis, and Gumbs." Just like junior high school, the five of us handed out the paper ballots and took them up.

Then we tellers sat around a small wooden table in a small windowless room above the Cathedral. We stared at Ken Price. He clutched a stack of white paper ballots in his hands and looked not at us but at the papers as if he were reluctant to let them go. Ken is short and overweight and close to retirement. I could see the beads of sweat on his forehead, but he wouldn't let go of the papers to wipe his brow.

"We are waiting for the Presiding Bishop's chancellor," he said in a voice loud enough to reveal his irritation.

A loud knock announced the arrival of a short man in a dark gray suit befitting a corporate lawyer. His glasses hung from a gold chain around his neck. "Let's go over the rules," he announced.

"Remember bishops, we have elected a Presiding Bishop in this manner twenty-five times in our history. We are Episcopalians so we have a set way of doing it. It may seem archaic to you, but it works."

I was back in third grade. It was important and I didn't want to screw it up.

"First," the chancellor continued, "I will assign roles. Then we will count the first ballot."

He looked around the table. Ambrose Gumbs, the Bishop of the Virgin Islands, sat next to him. In his forties, light brown skin, quiet, Caribbean accent.

"Bishop Gumbs. You will take the ballots, unfold them, smooth them carefully, and hand them one by one to Bishop Taylor."

"Bishop Taylor, you will read the name marked on the ballot aloud. If there are two names marked, the ballot is spoiled and will go in a different pile. If the ballot is valid, you will hand it to Bishop Steenson who will affirm your reading of the name.

"Bishop Steenson, you will simply say confirm or disagree and place the ballots in piles by name."

"Bishops Rivera and Mathis, you will mark separate tally sheets."

Even if it was third grade, we were extremely nervous. We were ensconced in this small room while the other 183 bishops waited in the church below us.

It took about thirty minutes. When we first finished the task, I had no idea about the results. Ted Gulick got fifteen votes. Neil Alexander had twenty-six. Henry Parsley had thirty-six. But Katharine Jefferts Schori had forty-four. *Forty-four.*

We sat stunned. Then Ken Price said in his officious voice, "Ninety-five to win. No winner. We vote again."

By the second ballot, Henry and Katharine were tied. After we passed out the third ballots, Nedi and I stood in the back with the other three teller bishops in the front.

"Well?" she said. "Still think she can't win?"

"I am a believer," I said, "and if she wins, I'll claim I voted for her all along."

"If we do the right thing, we'll not only do good for the church, we'll also make history."

I could feel the buzz as I took up the ballots. I noticed that many bishops had shifted seats. The diehard conservatives were clustering in the back. Some of the women had gathered in the middle right pews.

Ballot number three: Katharine sixty-eight; Henry sixty-three. We broke for lunch.

Though we all pledged not to bring in our phones, I could see one of the most conservative and adversarial bishops holding his phone to his ear with his right hand and waving his left hand up and down. Short with bushy eyebrows, and a mellow voice, he didn't look harmful, but I had learned not to trust him about anything. His desire to advocate for very conservative issues was so strong, I thought he was willing to do anything for his causes.

After ballot number four, one of the bishops whispered to me as we finished voting, "You won't believe this, but the arch conservatives are going to vote for Katharine."

I grabbed his arm. "That can't be true. Why would they do such a thing? They hate her and don't even believe in the ordination of women to the priesthood."

"Because they think it will sink the church and then they can mop up."

"Wait," I said, and grabbed his arm. "How do you know this?"

"Because," he said, "one of them showed me his ballot."

I was reeling. As a bishop I was privileged to meet people that I never would otherwise: Richard Rodriguez, Elisabeth Von Trapp, Miroslov Volf, Desmond Tutu. And I had opportunities to go places—London, Ecuador, San Francisco, the Virgin Islands, Puerto Rico, New York. But my naiveté was gone. Martin Luther said the church "is the Queen of Heaven and the Whore of Babylon." I couldn't stomach more Babylon. If I was going to represent an institution, I needed to believe in it. It was okay to disagree, but to lie and to do mischief?

I remembered that a year ago at a bishops' meeting, one of the conservative bishops did not tell the truth about one of his travels overseas.

He and some other bishops were playing on a chess board I didn't even know about. I couldn't follow their moves. They wouldn't ordain women, but they'd vote for a woman to head our church?

Thankfully, the task of counting cut my reverie short. The chancellor made us count ballot four twice. Katharine eighty-eight; Henry seventy-nine. Ninety-five to win. Neil was down to twelve.

When Frank Griswold, sitting at the table at the front of the church, read the results, a buzz erupted. Seven votes short. I heard the bishop in front of me say to no one and everyone, "Folks, do the math and you'll know what to do."

The bishops were quieter during the fifth vote. When we counters gathered in the room, Ken Price said, "If there is a winner, we are going to count these ballots three times."

I read the names slower than before. Our routine somehow took on a formality that was not there before. Ambrose Gumbs smoothed the ballots as if they were artifacts. The Presiding Bishop's chancellor stood behind Nedi and Jim Mathis to check their tallies.

When the stack was almost done, I heard Nedi suck in air. She didn't say anything, but she didn't have to.

"Is there an election?" Ken Price asked in a kind of sergeant-at-arms voice.

Jim Mathis said, "Katharine Jefferts Schori has the required ninety-five votes. We have an election."

"Whoa." That's what I heard myself say. Louder. "Whoa."

Nedi was shaking. Tears ran down her face. We all looked at one another as if we had discovered an ocean or a new continent. I came to General Convention because as a bishop I had to, but to my astonishment, we made history. The only part of the Anglican Communion with a woman in charge.

Katharine won with ninety-five votes—not a vote extra. Henry Parsley got eighty-two. Thirteen believers short.

Ken Price said, "Bishop Taylor, as the senior bishop here, you are to walk to the Presiding Bishop's table, and announce 'there is an election' and hand him the result sheet." His voice grew lower and louder, "None of you are to make any demonstration or indication in any way. Is that clear?"

We nodded like school children.

"Let's all just stare at the floor as we walk into the room," I said. "It'll be better."

As we stood, I grabbed Nedi's hand and squeezed it. I still couldn't do better than "Whoa."

As I walked down the stairs, I realized I felt hopeful about the church as an institution for the first time in at least a year. I had grown jaded and weary of all the maneuvering over who could gain the Archbishop of Canterbury's favor, or which dioceses were withholding money from the national church. I was tired of arguing and spending days and weeks in windowless banquet halls to vote on things that would not change anything except to inflate more egos.

I hated representing a country club male church. My son was dating a seminarian in New York. When I would visit, she'd ask me, "Are we going to get rid of having to call God a man this year?"

"Don't give up hope," I'd say, but in some sense I had. The church machine had ground me down. I came back to the church at twenty-nine because I felt a connection to a source, a power. Something opened me up when I stood around the altar at six-thirty on Friday morning and ate the bread of heaven. I wept because I didn't know how dead I was until I came alive.

But being a bishop was taking away that life force because every piece of paper I touched was not about the radical grace of God but about the church machine. I had lost a sense of a horizon. Here I was at fifty-six thinking about my pension and when I could do what I wanted to do—preach and pray and teach and pastor. I wanted to discover the holy with people who wanted to go deeper into things that mattered like wonder and pain and birth and death.

Katharine's election made my pulse race and my heart pound, and my throat choke up.

When we walked into the church, the crowd quieted and the bishops in the aisles hurried to their seats. I walked to where the Presiding Bishop sat and held the paper as if it were the Magna Carta. I leaned over and said in a hushed voice just loud enough for him to hear, "There is an election." I thought, "This is really the Presiding Bishop's moment not mine."

Bishop Griswold sat up straighter and said in a voice lower than usual. "There is an election. Let me remind the bishops, there is to be no cheering. We thank those who offered themselves for the election for their willingness to serve and be vulnerable in such a public way."

I lost Nedi but found a seat next to the bishop of Indianapolis. She and I became friends because we were both Yellow Dog Democrats. Her blonde hair gave her a kind of Meryl Streep look.

Frank Griswold read the results in ascending order.

No one was in double digits until he got to Henry.

"Henry Parsley eighty-two votes."

He paused. "Ninety-five votes are required for an election. Katharine Jefferts Schori ninety-five votes."

There was a quiet moment when the world stopped turning. No movement. No sound. Just the pause between the old order and the new.

Then the hall erupted. Most of the bishops stood and cheered. Cate Waynick reached to the pew in front of us and grabbed the bishop of Utah, Callie Irish, in a fierce hug. They both wept and laughed at the same time.

Some bishops sang "Praise God from whom all blessings flow."

I looked for Katharine and finally spotted her in the middle aisle. Her hands were over her mouth. Tears streamed down her face. A gravitational force brought the other eleven women bishops to her as they formed a circle with her in the middle aisle, their arms around one another's shoulders. They jumped up and down the way school children do when their energy overpowers their bodies. They too were laughing and crying.

When I looked in the back of the hall, I could see the conservative bishop wheeling himself out even though we were told we could not leave the hall. In the back corner another conservative bishop was talking on his cell phone.

Then the women scattered for a moment and moved to the front table where Frank Griswold had been sitting. They had their books—*Be It Remembered*—in their hands. Katharine sat and started signing.

And like slow learners, the men bishops queued up. I reached into my tote bag and waited my turn. "Katharine Jefferts Schori 6–18–06" she wrote.

Frank Griswold called us together by getting the organist to play "The Church's One Foundation."

He asked Katharine to speak, but she could not begin. She opened her mouth, but no words could come. Finally, she said something about being honored, humbled and the ministry of reconciliation, but she could have read the phone book, and we would have cheered.

We had to wait a long time in the church for the bureaucracy to make everything official. The flood of adrenalin left me spent.

When we emerged, there were already reporters outside the church. I took the bus back to the Convention Hall and walked down the hallway outside the auditorium where the clergy and lay representatives met. Our convention had two legislative bodies—bishops and "deputies." Bishops elected the Presiding Bishop, and deputies, about five hundred of them, confirmed elections. From the large hall, all I heard was the word "Katharine" and then a thunderous roar.

For a moment I thought about going in, but I couldn't hold any more.

Instead, I walked outside the Convention Hall through the sparsely populated streets of Columbus. It was a summer day with a slight wind.

I found myself at Goodale Park, a short distance from the hall. I walked around the lake. The swans swam in large circles with only the shortest ripple trailing behind them. Across the lake, children rushed down the slide or moved in rhythm on the swings. I could hear traces of their laughter. The trees rustled.

For the first time in a long time, I thought about going back to the diocese and work, and my step quickened.

# 12

## Where to Stand

*The deep suffering of the soul in the night of sense comes not so much from the aridity she must endure but from this growing suspicion that she has lost her way.*

—JOHN OF THE CROSS, *THE DARK NIGHT OF THE SOUL*

"WALK AROUND FEELING LIKE a leaf. / Know you could tumble any second. / Then decide what to do with your time."[1]

I looked at the ten seminarians in my Literature and Theology class. Five stared down at their books. Three avoided looking directly at me and two slowly nodded their heads.

"Amy, what does this passage from 'The Art of Disappearing' by Naomi Shihab Nye, say to you?"

She answered with her flat Texas accent. "It says to me that life is short and it's easy to waste it."

"Good. What about the image? What does it mean to walk around like a leaf?"

She curled her blonde hair with her right finger. "Well, I guess it means to feel the wind twirling you and while that force animates you, it can also bring your death."

I nodded. "Good. It's a Carpe Diem poem—seize the day. 'Gather ye rosebuds' and all that. But the poet isn't saying to live life to the fullest in

1. Nye, "The Art of Disappearing," 29.

129

a kind of bucket-list way. Rather, don't get mired in the trivial. 'Go deep' might be a paraphrase."

A bright twenty-five-year-old male from Virginia spoke. "Is this really a hazard in the church? I mean after all, we are dealing with sacred transitions in people's lives."

I didn't know what to say. Here I was teaching a class at Virginia Theological Seminary in Alexandria, Virginia, to these soon-to-be priests. Their naiveté came out often. Looking at them, I saw myself twenty years ago before the sometime pettiness of the work pressed much of that enthusiasm out.

"You'll be dealing with people where they are, and they'll be everywhere. The church is part of the world with all its stuff as well as its grace," I said. But my thought was, *talk to me in twenty years and see if the transitions you deal with feel sacred.*

As I walked back to the house allotted for us by the seminary, I tried to remember when I had felt that inspired about my calling. God knows, it was before I became a bishop. In my parish in Athens, Georgia, I loved giving spiritual direction to some of my parishioners. They would come into my office and talk about God's movements in their lives. "I have forgotten how to pray," they'd say. Or "When I walk in the woods, I feel this deep connectedness. Is that God's presence?" And we'd talk. These conversations were real and dear. They gave me a sense that I was aligned with where I was called to be because they weren't about finances or the Canons or petty church politics.

I came to Virginia Seminary for the month of February because I was worn out being the bishop. I was losing myself, and all those parts that gave me life. I was becoming less a shepherd and more the mayor or the police.

After two weeks of teaching, I sat with Jo at our small dining room table that was half covered by a newly started jigsaw—a Van Gogh painting of a Paris café. We had only connected the border. Jo said to me, "I feel as if you are finally back. It's been a long time since the person sitting across from me at the table is really you."

During our time in Alexandria, I lived for my three classroom hours with the students. I put my watch on the table at the first class. The student next to me asked why and I said, "Because I am afraid that I'll never want to stop." Each class I brought enough notes for an entire semester.

When I thought about returning to North Carolina and putting on my purple shirt, instead of feeling like a leaf, once more I feared becoming the trunk of the tree.

The night before we departed Virginia Seminary, we had dinner with a retired bishop and his wife. We met them at a seafood restaurant in the suburbs of Alexandria. Because it was Sunday, I knew the bishop had visited two churches that day and must be tired.

He and I are opposite in temperament, which may be why we like each other so much. I am moody; he is effervescent. I am distant; he loves church coffee hours. I think in images; he thinks in theological propositions. We are the same age, but he has been a bishop for seventeen years.

We sat in the booth and caught up. His wife is quiet and a dear soul. She and I trade novels at conferences.

"Are you going to Taiwan next year?"

"How are your kids?"

"So," my friend said in his sonorous voice, "how's it being the Bishop of Western North Carolina these days?" He leaned across the table with a wide grin. I felt as if he expected me to give some gem of ecclesial wisdom, but I had none. "Well," I said, and paused because I wasn't sure how deep to go. "Well." I felt a wave of emotion course through me. My throat got tight. "The truth is, I don't know if I can do this bishop thing anymore. I fear I am losing myself. Instead of feeling present, I feel like a stuffed shirt. The work's not hard; the priests who gave me trouble have quieted down. But I don't feel alive."

My friend went into a theological talk about resurrection. When he stopped, his wife said, "Why don't you do something else?"

Jo said, "That's what I keep saying. Here we are at VTS, and the students love Porter. He could teach here." I knew who her audience was. When she caught my eye, she raised her eyebrows and widened her eyelids as if to say, "Can you hear me now?"

"It's complicated," I said. "It's hard because trying to find a job while you are still the bishop is like trying to find a date while you are married. You can't exactly put the word out: 'I am restless and looking for a job.'"

We commiserated about the restraints of the office for a while and told stories of bishops who left suddenly or stayed too long. Jo was quiet.

Then my friend said in a kind of pronouncement, "I have an idea. There's a cardinal church that's coming open. Let me talk to the bishop and I'll see what we can do. You'd be a perfect interim there, and it pays well."

"How well is well?" Jo asked.

"Trust me," he said. "Porter will make a bucketful more there than he does now."

On our drive home, Jo wrapped her hands around my right arm and leaned into me as I steered. "Bam, this sounds like a way to get our life back. Promise me you'll try. Promise."

"It's not in my court, Jo. If the bishop phones me, I will more than try. I promise."

* * *

In March, our diocese held its Lenten Retreat for clergy at Valle Crucis Conference Center near Boone, North Carolina. I invited a retired monk from St. John the Evangelist Monastery in Cambridge Massachusetts to be our speaker. He is bean-pole tall. At the opening session he stood in his black cassock before the two dozen priests and wrapped his arms around his chest as he talked.

"Thank you for all you do for the Lord," he began in a high reedy voice. Then he closed his eyes when he talked and tilted his head almost as if he were talking to the heavens. "Thank you for living a holy life. Thank you for caring for the sick, listening to the lonely, comforting those who mourn. Thank you."

He lowered his head and scanned the room, thanking us with his gaze. For the next two hours he talked about leading a prayerful life in a noisy world. Afterward I stood waiting near the wall for the crowd to clear. I asked if I could talk to him one on one.

"The walls of the bishop bubble get thicker and thicker every year," I said the next morning as we sat facing one another. We rocked in our rocking chairs and looked across the valley to the newly green hills. "I don't have any friends because people are allergic to purple shirts. And I am getting jaded. I hate the pettiness and the politics. Last week I was told I had financially ruined the diocese and that I had sold out the church to the gay and lesbian lobby. All in one week. I am in a box and it's too small."

"Porter, why do you think this is about you? It's just the cost of wearing a uniform," he said. We looked across the valley with two John Deere tractors left in the middle of the hay field.

"Let's try a different way," he said. "What do you love about your job?"

"I love preaching and teaching. I guess there's a part of me that still wants to be Elvis. I like what happens in the pulpit, and I like what happens when I play with ideas."

"And?"

"And look at the places I have been—England, Taiwan, Ecuador, Scotland. I've met the Queen of England and I'm on a first-name basis with the Presiding Bishop. Me. And I decide who is ordained and I ordain them."

I turned and looked at him. "I am grateful, I really am. I never thought I'd do any of this."

"But," he said. "You are afraid it's taking your life away."

"Yes. That's it. Yes."

He stopped talking, turned his chair and leaned toward me. "Do you still connect with God's love for you? Is that a reality in your life?"

"In moments it is, but being a bishop makes it harder."

"Then you have to overcome that. You have to find that first love."

I shook my head. "I don't know if I can do this job and remember God's love. Half the time, I forget who I am apart from the role."

He bent his head closer until our heads almost touched and whispered, "All the saints had to slay their dragons and you have to slay yours. These voices are mirrors of what is choking your heart, but they're not from God."

"How do you slay them?"

"You let God love you. Then the dragons have no power. Do you believe God loves you?" he asked in a whisper.

"Yes," I said soft and slow, "and I don't think God wants me to be so unhappy."

He didn't say anything. When he did speak, his voice caught. "I don't either. But Porter, you know the problem isn't the job, don't you? The dragon isn't out there." He paused. "But here," and he tapped my chest.

"I know, but in the blur the dragons get bigger."

A week later I got a silver letter opener with a dragon on the handle. The note simply said, "Slay the dragon."

\* \* \*

I didn't hear anything about the Virginia parish for three months. Just as I was forgetting about it, the call came. On a Saturday afternoon in July, I was writing my sermon in the dining room of our home in Asheville. Jo was in the garden cutting back the brown leaves on her iris. The bishop in charge of the church called my cell phone. He got to the point quickly. "Porter, I have a proposition for you. We need an interim at one of our historic parishes. You'd be perfect."

He told me about the parish: progressive, big into social justice, generous salary, great choir, historic building.

"Let me know in a month or so," he said, before hanging up.

When I walked out to the garden and told Jo, she took off her gloves and put her hands on her cheeks and almost shouted, "Oh, Bam I am so excited. It sounds perfect."

"We'll see. You know it's not just about the place or the money. It's always about the people and the match." I rearranged my calendar, and in early August we drove to Virginia.

\* \* \*

"Jo, it's way too protestant for me. White walls, white pews, white pulpit. No color in the windows either."

We were thirty minutes early for the ten o'clock service at the church in Northern Virginia. A woman dressed in a white linen pantsuit ushered us to our seats four rows from the front. The pews had doors on the sides with numbers. I wore a white shirt and one of my two ties—the red one with blue polka dots. Today I wasn't a bishop but just a visitor.

The usher said, "I am so glad you are with us today," but the building itself didn't seem too glad. It was built in the late eighteenth century. People claimed that George Washington and Robert E. Lee attended. It was a classic colonial church.

For me it lacked color. Then there was the space itself. The altar was a small table that was literally overshadowed by the pulpit directly above it. The pulpit was an enormous white structure that reminded me of one of the Pope's balconies over St. Peter's square. The preacher could see eye to eye with the people in the balconies but would have to peer over the pulpit to see those below.

"I don't know," I whispered to Jo. "It's the most protestant Episcopal church I have ever seen. The focus should be on the altar and the Eucharist not the sermon, for God's sake."

"Hush," she said. "Number one, someone will hear you, and number two, no one's talking about forever. It's an interim position."

But I couldn't get comfortable. My internal dialog kept saying, *this is all wrong.* When the first reader came forward to read the lesson, she stood behind a small lectern that looked like it belonged in an elementary school. *Who's going to see her?* I thought because she was eye level with the congregation.

The rector didn't wear the right vestments—at least for me. He had on a black cassock and white surplice—which made him look like Bing Crosby. *It's the long green season in the church. He should be wearing green vestments.*

His sermon wasn't great. He read it, so it really didn't matter if he was twenty feet above us, but his voice was thin.

Jo felt me fidgeting and grabbed my leg with her hand to stop it from bouncing. "Be still," she whispered.

The choir was good. I noticed that the church was only two thirds full. Summer?

When I knelt for communion, the assistant rector put the bread in my hand as she said, "The body of Christ, the bread of heaven." I stared at my palm, and the surroundings disappeared for a moment. "Amen," I said.

After the service, Jo and I went to coffee hour in the Parish Hall—another antiseptic building. One woman in a professional gray suit came over with a big smile, but when we told her we were just visiting, she seemed to lose interest. We talked to the rector for a few minutes. He was polished but not really present. "So glad you are here. If you are looking for a church home, there's plenty going on here." But even as he said this, he was moving away.

"Well? What do you think?" Jo asked as we walked away from the church.

"I am trying to see myself here, but it's a challenge. First, some people look like bureaucrats. Second, the space just lacks color. It makes me want to mark on the walls or wear a red suit. And I can't image preaching in that pulpit so far up in the air."

"Well, you need to find out if you could preach there. Why don't you go back into the church and see what it's like?"

So, I did. No one was inside. The rail around the altar was closed with a sign saying, "Do Not Enter," but I ignored it and climbed over the rail and up the circular steps into the high pulpit. I looked straight across at the organ and the choir loft. The walls around me looked like a white dry erase board. Looking down I could imagine the upturned faces looking at me as if I were Captain Ahab. It felt as if I would be powerful and detached—and I knew neither would be good for my soul. I tended to perform in the pulpit anyway—to get my voice louder and to develop a cadence to my lines. My exterior preaching self didn't need any encouragement. *I'm already removed enough from the congregations. I don't need to elevate myself any higher.*

One of our friends recommended we visit the Torpedo Factory, an art school and exhibit hall in Old Town Alexandria. Inside there were maybe fifty small studios. Art everywhere. As usually happens, I was finished browsing way before Jo. I could see her bend to get closer to the paintings, her blonde hair hanging down and almost brushing the canvas. Then she leaned backward, pursed her lips, squinted her eyes, and stayed motionless as if she and the canvas were communing with one another. I was content to walk straight through the spaces, but Jo picked up things from the pottery exhibits and scrutinized the sculptures to see how they were made.

When we sat down to dinner, I said, "You first," because all our moves had focused on my career. If I were to take this job, the decision needed to be about her.

"This place is so alive. The Torpedo Factory has tons of art classes— painting, pastels, printmaking—it's all here."

She took a breath and then smiled a deep smile that I hadn't seen in a while. Jo reached out and put her hands on mine. "We could be so happy here. There's so much life. Can you see yourself at that church? Can you?"

"I don't know. I am sure the people are nice, and they say they are into outreach and the kind of causes I stand for. But Jo, the space feels so empty to me. The pulpit is too high, and the altar is too small. I don't know."

"Will you at least try to imagine us here? Please."

"Of course," I said, but I already felt myself resisting.

* * *

"What is it that binds you from making a free decision?" I sat across from my spiritual director. We met in his home study. He leaned back in his desk chair and locked his hands behind his head. He was in his late seventies and was a kind of Gandalf figure for me. He had his own scars from being the pastor of a liberal Baptist church. Unlike my past spiritual directors, he liked to talk about church systems and the connections between those and family systems. He once told me, "The way you deal with the bullies in your diocese mirrors your family system."

"That's bad news," I confessed.

"Porter? What binds you?"

"Oh. Well, it's a bunch of things, but there are two strong ones. First, there's the fear of being seen as a failure. Of sneaking away in the middle of the night."

After too long a pause, he prodded. "Where does that come from?"

"I dunno. Well, I do know. I just don't like it. Sometimes when I feel bad about myself, I just disappear. The best example is my football career. I played at North Carolina for two weeks, but as a walk-on, I didn't get to play much so I just packed my bags and got on a bus and went home."

"And?" he asked. "Where's the regret in that?"

"I always wondered what would have happened. Was I good enough to play? I told myself I came to college to get an education, but was that true or just a smoke screen?"

I remembered leaving the football dorm and sitting in the bus station in Chapel Hill. I was seventeen years old. I had gotten discouraged but mainly I was lonely. I was in a high-rise dormitory far from downtown. My roommate was a guy from Richmond who quit three days earlier. I came back from practice and his side of the room was empty. I was never a jock. I liked the flow of the game. As a split end, I was on the edge of the violence on the line itself.

One day after practice, an interior voice just said to me, "You don't belong here," and I decided to leave. I didn't call my parents. I wrote a note to Coach Spooner, the end coach, and left it on his door.

I waited a while in the bus station, and then Coach Spooner came in and sat beside me. He had a rough face—ravages from teenage acne, and a deep voice.

"Don't do this Taylor. You've got a fine future. Things will pick up for you. You need to trust me."

I didn't really hear him. I was done. "I can't do this Coach. I'm sorry. I want a normal college life."

Finally, we both stood up and he said, "I have one thing to tell you."

*Wow. He's going to wish me well.*

"You will regret this for the rest of your life," he said, and then he walked out the door.

The coach was wrong about those regrets, but what about this choice? Was I sneaking away to Virginia in the middle of the night? What about the reaction I'd get this time when the word was out?

My director said, "Porter, what's the second thing that binds you?"

"It's my staff. Every day I work with six people that I hired because I believed in them. They have become my congregation."

When he asked me what that meant, I told him about last summer. Our financial officer had a brother who died of a heart attack while jogging. He was fifty-three. He had a wife and three teenage children.

When I heard that the funeral was in Rock Hill, South Carolina, on Wednesday afternoon, I told the staff, "We're going." So, the five of us packed into my assistant's Highlander and drove to Rock Hill—just below Charlotte.

The funeral was in a contemporary church—a metal building with a sanctuary that looked like a movie theater. Cushy seats, big stage, speakers, drum set, and a screen that showed rotating images of her brother.

We sat on the third row. The brother had been a big supporter of the high school football team. He ran the concession stand for six years. The proceeds paid for new football equipment and uniforms. Before the service started, the whole football team filed in wearing their yellow jerseys. The preacher talked about our coworker's brother and his dedication to the football team.

"And to show his family how much he meant to the team, these young men are dedicating the season to our deceased brother, and they will wear this decal on their helmets all year." He held up a small circular yellow football decal with the brother's initials on it.

I wondered how many would remember me that way if I left. I thought about this man's willingness to stay dedicated to the thing he believed in, even if it was high school football.

The preacher wound up by saying he was glad the brother was saved so that we knew where he was and that if anyone here wasn't saved, now was the time to accept Jesus.

Then the eldest son talked. All my judgments about the church dissolved. He cried for the loss of his father. He said, "I hope I can be half the man he was."

*I am a judgmental jerk. Loss is loss is loss.*

When it was over, we waited in the lobby for our coworker. She came out surrounded by her family. Her face was ashen and hollow. Her mascara was smeared. When she saw us, she ran over and grabbed me—crying in sobs. "I can't believe you came," she stuttered.

"Of course, we came," I said. "We're family."

I finished my account to my director by saying, "I am bound to those people. I have a hard time walking out on them."

"Porter, let me tell you a story. When the Buddhist monks fled Tibet and walked into India, many of the monks gathered around the Dali Lama to travel with him. But the Dali Lama turned to them and said, 'Brothers, from now on we all walk with our own two feet.'" He paused, staring at me. "This is the only life you have to live. You can't spend it thinking of other people."

There was a truth there that I didn't want to hear, but it wasn't the whole truth.

"I don't want to be Edward VII and just walk out," I said a little louder than I intended. "I took vows and I think those mean something."

"Of course, they do. They mean you have to be faithful to what God is calling you to do to serve the Lord, but only you know what that is." When he finished saying this, he smiled.

I said, "Shit. I am sure that's right, but it doesn't help much."

\* \* \*

A few weeks later, near the end of August, Jo and I went to Pawley's Island for two weeks. In the morning we walked on the beach. Jo picked up shells and handed them to me to put in my bathing suit pockets. We sat under the umbrella. I read *Sacred Fire* by Ron Rolheiser. Jo read another Tana French mystery.

We tried not to talk about the church or our children, but most days we failed. Our daughter was underemployed, and our son faced financial problems. I always wanted to escape those topics during our time at the beach, but we ended up talking about them anyway.

"I don't want to walk out on those people, and I don't feel done there," I said.

"Is that you or is that your duty pulling you?"

"How do you separate those?"

One morning as we sat in our beach chairs under our umbrella, I read Rolheiser's book. He wrote about his nephew who worked on an oil rig. His nephew was twenty-two the day a cable snapped, hit him, and killed him.

Rolheiser wrote, "Loading grain cars was his job, and when the cable snapped and killed him, he was standing where he was supposed to be standing at that moment...Ultimately, that is all we can try to assure for ourselves. We can try to be standing where we are supposed to be standing... We can be at our post, in commitment, love, and duty. In the end, that is all we can do, and in the end, that is enough."[2]

The words jumped off the page. I felt convicted. Being in Northern Virginia would be fun and kind of glamorous. We would mingle with important people. Jo could take art lessons. We could go to the National Gallery once a week, but was that why I got ordained?

I remember one of the saints saying, "Look for God where you lost God." I also remembered this saint was burned by the church, but that's a different point. I doubted that moving was the solution to the issue that ailed me.

Jo was still reading Tana French. "Jo," I said. "I don't think I can do this."

"Do what?" she asked as she left her book and twisted to see me.

"Leave like this. It feels as if I am running out. I know one of my fears is disappointing people, but this just doesn't feel right. I don't want to be the guy who ditched the diocese for a better date. That's not how I want to be remembered."

"But you do admit this job is killing you. You do admit that don't you?" Her nurse directness.

"Yes. But if we are going to leave, let's find a different way, and maybe there's a way to make this work. After all, if I keep my pants on and don't steal money, no one's going to get rid of me."

When she didn't laugh, I said, "It's a joke. Let me try again. What do you need for me to stay?"

"You need to take care of your health. You need to slow down. You need to have fun. And we need time together. Since we haven't found out how to do those in ten years, are we going to do them now?"

I breathed a long breath out. "I don't know."

---

2. Rolheiser, *Sacred Fire*, 273–75.

We stared at the ocean for a while.

"Look," she said. "You are who you are, and I love who you are. You just aren't the kind of person to leave. I get that, but I can't watch you kill yourself. So, you will have to change things." We looked at each other. Finally, she smiled at me. "At least say you'll try to change things."

"I'll try."

We walked down the beach. Vacationers were settling in. Children were making castles. Men with flat stomachs were throwing bocce balls. People were reading and talking. Like them, Jo and I had found a place in between. We had found a place outside the daily drill and for a moment outside either/or.

I was relieved not to go to the Virginia church. It would have been a smart move, but it didn't fit me, not because of any noble qualities on my part. It just wasn't who I was. I had severed enough connections in my life. I didn't want to sever any more.

Part of me wished I hadn't been called to be the Bishop of Western North Carolina, but I had been. This is where I had to stand until I could move somewhere else in the daylight, not in the middle of the night. Leaving felt like a cheat to me. A quick fix with a long regret.

But that didn't fix my condition. I knew that, but for the moment, Jo and I walked down the beach between the ocean and the road.

# 13

## Michael Curry

Behold I am in all things.
Behold I accomplish all things.
Behold I never withdraw my arms from my work.
Behold I never fail to guide all things
Toward the purpose for which I created them,
Before time began,
With strength, wisdom, and love,
With which I created all.
So how can anything go wrong?

—JULIAN OF NORWICH, *ALL WILL BE WELL*

"AM I IN THE right place?" I asked a woman wearing a red vest with a card labeled "Volunteer" dangling from a lanyard on her chest. I peered into the vast concrete room packed with people and reverberating with the sound of excited voices.

She looked at the purple badge around my neck, then smiled and said, "Yes, bishop. Welcome to the House of Deputies. The program starts right at one thirty, so you've got about fifteen minutes."

It didn't look like a house. It looked like an underground bunker that could shelter an entire city from a nuclear strike. The hall was enormous, packed with people and divided into two sections. The outer section had rows and rows of chairs and behind them a throng of people talking, laughing, clustering.

As I walked in, I approached a man who was also wearing a red vest. "I'm Porter Taylor, the bishop of Western North Carolina. Any idea where I belong?"

He pointed to the far end of the hall. "Walk ahead and you'll see the gate into the Deputies Section. There's a map of the tables by diocese. You'll find where you need to be."

I had come to the General Convention. This year we were in Salt Lake City, and I had arrived the afternoon before. I was tired. While my body was still on Eastern time, it had decided that four a.m. was an appropriate time to rise. The convention was scheduled for nine days, which ought to be plenty of time to do our business. After all, God created the world in seven, but this wasn't even day one. Today was "Orientation Day."

The Episcopal Church elects its leader, the Presiding Bishop, every nine years and this was the year we'd elect a new one. The hall was packed today because the four nominees for Presiding Bishop were to be introduced and answer questions. The hall looked like a harbor with boats battened down for the winter. There must have been three thousand people in the room. I wandered through the sea of tables, each with a pole identifying the diocese, and looked for Western North Carolina. There are 109 dioceses in the church; each diocese had eight deputies on the floor.

"Porter, we're here." A woman from our diocese, called to me and waved me over. Our table was about halfway back from the speakers' platform. I had to lean down to talk to her because the noise was deafening.

"Are you sorry this is your last convention?" she asked as I sat down. Her voice was raspy.

"No and no. I'm just sorry that we have nine more days in these air hangar rooms with no windows." In April, I had announced that I was retiring as the bishop of Western North Carolina. A new bishop would be elected in the summer of 2016 and take office that October. It hadn't been easy for me to get into office, nor would it be easy to get out.

I thought about the four bishop nominees and their qualifications and wondered if I had those qualities that brought them here. Would I have stayed for the long haul? I doubted it. I had an impatience about bureaucracy, an aversion to what felt like time-wasting enterprises like these conventions, and a sickness over the political games that are required to be effective.

I was also tired. Tired of the endless meetings, the conflict, the pettiness of church politics that kept me in the suburbs of God's heart, driving around the interstate loop outside the city central. I wanted to unload so that maybe I could make my way to the heart of things without all the baggage that comes with the office. Most of all, I was tired of not having a community. When I was a parish priest, I preached to the same people week in, week out, and we developed a kind of conversation. We knew each other's lives, and for me there was a corollary between intimacy with people and intimacy with God. But the longer I wore the purple bishop's shirt, the farther I moved away from the connection I sorely needed with other people, with God, and with my truer self. People joked about losing your first name when you are elected, because everyone just calls you "Bishop," but after eleven years, it wasn't funny anymore.

Yet, I was no martyr, nor a victim. As much as I grumbled about the travel, I loved being with such a wide variety of people. I went to parishes that had four hundred people on Sunday, and some that had twelve. I loved that with only a few exceptions, people were glad, even honored, to see me. When I came to visit, it was important.

Regardless of the wear and tear of being a bishop, it was also a great privilege and joy. In eleven years, I had been all over the globe and met very interesting people. I had been blessed to be given this role. However, the blessing was robbing me of who I was. A part of me envied the four bishops on the stage, not that I wanted to be Presiding Bishop, but I wanted their confidence and sense of direction. I had grown tired of my capacity to conform to what the system required, but I didn't know any way to change except to get out.

The Episcopal Church was in the midst of an identity shift. Our name means that the "episcopacy," or bishop, is at our center, yet we live in an age that suspects hierarchy. Nine years ago, the nominees for the Presiding Bishop met solely with the bishops to answer questions. This made sense to me because bishops elect the Presiding Bishops, and the Deputies confirm the election. However, what made sense in 2006 no longer made sense to many people in the church in 2015. Therefore, the nominees were announced after our March bishops' meeting—too late for the bishops to have a private interview. Instead, the four nominees were to be questioned before everyone. This meant the bishops had only three days between the interview forum and the vote. I wondered if the point was to remind the church of our bicameral system. The bishops weren't the only ones who got access to the nominees.

In the Convention Hall a priest came to the podium and asked us to be seated and to be quiet. He was tall, African American, and spoke with a tenor voice.

"I'm from Hawaii," he said. "Welcome." He told us we would see a video each candidate had prepared. There were four candidates: Tom Bridenthal from Southern Ohio, Michael Curry from North Carolina, Ian Douglas from Connecticut, and Dabney Smith from Southeast Florida. All of them were smart, accomplished, and electable. But one of them, Michael Curry, could become the first African American to head our denomination.

I had known Michael Curry since I was ordained a bishop in 2004. He was different from me. He loves to talk to people; he loves to eat and joke and laugh; and he loves the church machine. He's a good politician and pastor. When he gets near people, he leans into them, so they feel as if they are the only other person in the room. Maybe that's why Michael was getting farther into church land, and I was getting out. My strengths were teaching and preaching. I could inspire people and come alive in the pulpit or classroom. However, I disliked the rough and tumble of church politics. Instead of arguing to get someone to do what I wanted them to do, I'd ask them what books they'd read, and skirt around the subject.

Each nominee had made a video to introduce them to the Convention. The videos were sweet, somewhat dorky but endearing. At the beginning of Tom Bridenthal's video, he and his wife Margaret were walking down the sidewalk from their home in Cincinnati to a coffee shop. He talked about his visions for the church and what he'd done with his diocese in Southern Ohio. He wore blue jeans and a sports shirt. When he ordered a double espresso, I wondered if that was to inject him with a jolt of energy for the video, or if espresso was his normal drink. He spoke of the ecological efforts he had initiated and mentioned his love of Byzantine art history. This underscored my conviction that he was the smartest bishop I knew. A former chaplain of Princeton, he was articulate and a sweet soul. I loved Tom. In fact, when I first thought about resigning from being the bishop, Tom was the person I called for advice.

Michael Curry's video began with him standing in his dark suit and purple shirt in front of St. Augustine's Chapel in Raleigh, a modest brick church built in 1867. He talked about getting over our Episcopal aversion to evangelism. He was warm and engaging, but not vintage Michael Curry. On tape, the energy didn't flow out of him as it did when he preached. Maybe this was because he had to stand still, unable to move around or shuffle his feet as he did when he was wound up in the pulpit.

Ian Douglas, Bishop of Connecticut, had salt and pepper hair. When he talked, his New England accent was evident. He stood in a parking lot in front of a large brick building. I heard car sounds as he told us that his diocese had left its expensive mansion to relocate to the center of Hartford. The video reminded us he was from a city, and not afraid to stir things up.

The Bishop of Southeast Florida, Dabney Smith, presented the most touching video. He stood with his new wife in front of a church with the Manatee River behind them. He wore a tan suit and talked about his father being a priest. Then he showed a picture of his father with the bishop of that diocese in the 1960s and himself as a toddler playing on the floor. This meant he was steeped in the church, and we could trust him.

After the videos, the lights came up and I could see the four candidates behind a long rectangular table draped in a shiny blue tablecloth. In fact, the whole stage was covered in this material, making it look like a stage set for high school graduation. The master of ceremonies came to the podium to give instructions to the four men on stage. "In front of you is a bowl with colored slips of paper," he said. "There are eight colors, and each one stands for a different topic. The topics are leadership, theology/liturgy, faith-based issues, LGBTQ, structure, divestment, spiritual life, and reconciliation. You are to draw one slip but be sure that each of you draws a different color for each round. You will have two minutes to answer the question. We'll begin with Bishop Smith. I ask the audience to refrain from any applause."

Dabney Smith held up a blue paper he had drawn from the bowl and said "blue four" as if we were playing bingo. I didn't hear the question or the answer because I was trying to figure out the logic of this system, especially the correlation between the colors and the topics. Was there something especially blue about LGBTQ issues? Did red and structure always go together? Was this the way maps were constructed? Argentina is always yellow? Canada is always pink?

When Michael Curry came to the platform, he was asked a question about reconciliation, a green question. He said, "In the love of Jesus there is room for all of us," and paused. Then his voice lowered as he said, "As a bishop, I am not the pope." And then he kind of shook his head and chuckled, adding, "Well, the pope isn't the pope either." The room roared. "Jesus does love us all and because of that we can be in relationship and be real."

In that moment, I felt sure that Michael Curry would be elected. All along I'd thought he would, but my confidence grew because even in this vast room, he connected with people and reassured them that they were important. Therefore, they could trust him. The other three nominees gave terrific answers but did not connect and offer reassurance in the same way.

Tom Bridenthal was asked about divesting from investments in Palestine, a tan question. I said to myself, "Good luck with that topic," because I knew nothing about investments or the latest in the conflict with Palestine and Israel. He took a moment before responding and stood straight in his dark gray suit. When he talked, he often touched his forefinger with his thumb to make a point. As he spoke about this topic, he became more excited about the idea and his speech grew faster and slightly louder. I tried to write down what he said because I knew he was right. Tom was always right.

He said, "We don't need to sever our ties; we need to strengthen them," and I nodded my head.

Perhaps the sweetest moment was when Dabney Smith was asked an orange question, "Do you believe in the resurrection?" In response, he blurted, "Oh my God, thank you," and we laughed because we thought he was happy to have such an easy question. However, he told of his first wife's death during Holy Week and how as the Good Friday liturgy followed Jesus to the cross, so he had to wade into his deep grief but found resurrection on the other side. "The resurrection is the truth," he said. "And the truth is Jesus is alive." I was proud to be his friend. I didn't think he would be elected because he was too conservative, but I would have been proud to serve him.

After all the questions were answered, each nominee made a closing statement. Ian Douglas thanked everyone, including the discernment committee and his fellow nominees. When he thanked his diocese, his voice choked up and I realized the difference between being an observer and being part of the Body. I had been watching these the way you watch television, but Ian's emotion again reminded me that these were life and blood brothers, who had been through an exhausting process.

Michael talked about a funeral of a youth shot in Baltimore when he was a parish priest. As the coffin was being lowered into the ground, one of the Black teenagers said, "We'll see you real soon." His voice hoarse with emotion, Bishop Curry said, "We have a message to proclaim to the world and we need to go out in the name of the Lord and end this nightmare."

Tom Bridenthal talked about Pentecost and the creativity and courage and patience required to do something new. He spoke without notes and with the same passion he brought to everything.

Dabney Smith ended on a nostalgic note. He talked about going to church as a boy right after Hurricane Donna and feeling the safety of the sanctuary as the storm raged outside. It was genuine and sincere and endearing.

I had such a deep admiration for those four. This session had lasted three hours. I had trouble being coherent for a fifteen-minute sermon and I controlled the subject. I couldn't imagine being asked random questions for that long.

\* \* \*

Three days later on a hot Friday morning, June 26, I walked into St. Mark's Cathedral. Under my black suit coat the sweat made my purple bishop's shirt stick to my back. But I wasn't thinking about the heat of Salt Lake City, where our convention was being held, or the scenic sites I could be seeing in the Utah mountains. Instead, my mind was on a future I would shape. I was one of 174 bishops who would elect the next Presiding Bishop of The Episcopal Church on this day.

The church was not spacious, because after all, we were in the land of Mormons. No need for a large Episcopal church here. The murmurs of the bishops bounced off the dark stained walls and became a white noise that did not cure the tension I felt. I was excited to be part of this election, but my excitement was dampened by doubts about my own accomplishments in my episcopacy. I was haunted by thoughts of having been too safe, too calculated, too confined by the office. It felt as if I stood at a crossroads—on the verge of making history in this election, even as I knew that in retirement I was headed for the sidelines.

As I looked around the room, I knew I'd miss all these people and this community of bishops. However, sitting in windowless, vacuous convention halls for ten days talking about the church's position on subjects as diverse as liturgies for pet blessings to climate change to insurance policies, was not how I envisioned my future. I didn't think I was above it; I had just lost the patience for it.

I entered the Cathedral sanctuary at the back of the line but kept moving up the aisle as other bishops settled for the cheap seats. Nine years ago, at the Convention in Columbus, Ohio, when the first female Presiding Bishop, Katharine Jefferts Schori, was elected, I sat with Nedi Rivera, the bishop from Eastern Oregon. Nedi waved to me from the front row. Since a miracle had happened in electing Katharine, she and I didn't want to block the Holy Spirit by changing our seats. Walking up the center aisle of the crowded Cathedral, I surveyed a sea of purple shirts and black suits. The walls of the chancel were a cream color that set off the dark brown beams of the vaulted ceiling. On the right side behind the altar was a stained-glass window of Jesus transfigured—with radiant light coming from him. The window to the left showed the angel coming to Mary to give her the shocking news. I noticed Mary's right hand reached for the ground to keep her balance and wondered if this day would resemble that drama.

"I have to help count the votes, so we get to sit on the front row," Nedi said as she reached out to hug me. I loved her. She had a California freeness that I sorely lacked. Her red polished fingernails and bright gold loop earrings made me feel especially Amish. Her whoop of a laugh always put me at ease, and her generous heart gave me hope.

"What do you think?" I said to her, leaning over to keep our pre-election predictions private.

"Well, you know I love all of them, but this is Michael's day."

"You're so right," I said.

As I sat in the front row of the Cathedral with Nedi, waiting to vote, I wondered how those who weren't elected would fit back into their lives. Could they reenter the picture they presented in the videos three days earlier, or would the ideas of what could have been pinch them as they tried to get back into their former lives? And what narrative did I think I would enter once I extracted myself from being a bishop?

At the front of St. Mark's Cathedral was a white table. As the head of the church, Bishop Katharine Jefferts Schori sat in the middle, surrounded by assisting bishops looking very proper. They looked like some kind of ecclesial tribunal with their mix of purple and dark suits. Katharine had on her business face. No smiles, no small talk, her direct laser eyes scanning the room.

She called on the chaplains: The Rev. Stephanie Spellers and the Rev. Simone Bautista, but only Simone stood because Stephanie had broken her leg dancing in Bermuda the week before. In her defense, Stephanie was the only person in the room under thirty-five, and maybe the only one who could dance in a bar and not look foolish. Simone is from Trinidad and has a beautiful island lilt. Tall, wiry, and Black, he towered over the bishops sitting at the head table as he read from Ephesians 4:11–12: "The gift that he gave is that some would be apostles . . . to equip the saints for the work of the ministry, for building up the body of Christ . . . "

There was a long silence in the room, a silence in which the Spirit began to blow the world one way or another. Then Stephanie stood, propped with her crutch, and began singing in her soprano voice, "Veni Sanctus Spiritus," over and over until we bishops joined in. This chant is sung in ordinations just before a bishop's hands go on the ordinand's head. I closed my eyes as I sang and prayed for the Holy Spirit not just to come to this gathering, but to come to me and show me the way. The bishops continued chanting "Veni Sanctus Spiritus," as Stephanie sang the verses in her strong bold voice.

> Come Holy Spirit, Shine forth with your Glorious Light.
> Come from the four winds, O Spirit come.
> Breath of God disperse the shadows over us, renew and strengthen your people.
> Guardian of the poor, come to our poverty.
> Shower upon us the seven-fold gifts of your grace. Be the light of our lives.[1]

There was a long silence, a time when it felt as if everything paused because something important would happen. Maybe history would be made if Michael were elected. A gentle excitement ran through me. At the last

1. Berthier, *Veni Sanctus Spiritus*, 68–70.

election nine years ago, I thought it mattered which of the nominees got elected, but this time, I thought any of the four would do well. Maybe not all would be great, but they would be fine because as bishops we all learn how to administrate, preside at ceremonial functions, and cast a vision.

However, only Michael would be the one who could make history, and I needed some act to renew my faith in the institution of the church. I still loved the Lord. I sometimes felt God's presence. I believed in the divine power to make the world new, but late at night, I wondered if Jesus was in despair over the stiffness and emptiness of the church. I wondered if he shared my impatience for us to get to what matters in people's lives, instead of playing at some ecclesial parliament. I loved the pastoral parts of the job, but they were small in comparison to the meetings I had to chair or attend. I was still awed by being a bishop, but in this office my soul was slowly leaking out of me. I knew in my head that having an African American as the leader of the church wouldn't solve the restlessness that was moving me on, nor would it magically fix the church, but in my heart, I yearned for something to inspire me about the church again. Electing Michael Curry might do that.

After the chant in her calm Oregon voice, Bishop Katharine said this prayer:

> *O God of unchangeable power and eternal light: Look favorably on your whole church, that wonderful and sacred mystery; by the effectual working of your providence, carry out in tranquility the plan of your salvation; let the whole world see and know that things which had been cast down are being raised up, and things which had grown old are being made new, and all things are being brought to their perfection by him through whom all things were made, your Son Jesus Christ our Lord; who lives and reigns with you, in the unity of the Holy Spirit, one God, for ever and ever. Amen.*[2]

"Amen and Amen," I said softly, because I knew too many of us needed to be made new, especially me. The holy quietness that followed was broken by a spokesperson for the church machine, making sure we didn't screw up the election. The Secretary of the House of Bishops called the roll, which meant he called the name of every bishop who was eligible to vote, whether they were present or not. He must have gone through fifteen names—few of whom I recognized—before he got to "David Reed," the longest serving bishop who was present. About ten minutes later I heard "Bishop of Western North Carolina," and duly responded, "Here" just like in high school.

Bishop Katharine gave us instructions about outside communication, as if we were school children: "No texting, no phoning, no tweeting. After

2. *The Book of Common Prayer*, 515.

the balloting, everyone has to stay in the building. Let's respect all the nominees during this time."

I remembered the election of Bishop Katharine in 2006, and there was none of that kind of anxiety in this room. On that day, the discord between the conservative and liberal bishops tainted the atmosphere, but none of that was present on this day.

I saw that one of the nominees was sitting across the aisle from me and looked tense, but then again, I was tense, and I wasn't even on the ballot.

We were handed a yellow paper scorecard for the ballots, with columns for eleven rounds of voting. Old school.

"Vote for one."

I put a check in the box by Michael Curry's name, folded it and handed it to Sean Rowe, the youngest bishop in the church, at thirty-eight.

Then we waited for the votes to be counted. Bishops got out of their pews and meandered out of the church to use the bathroom.

Nedi was a teller, so she left to count. I walked around until I saw a friend.

"What do you think?" he asked.

"It's not what's going to happen; it's only when," I answered, because I was confident that Michael would be elected.

"This is Michael's day," he agreed.

Being around Michael Curry thawed me out of my habitual frozen respectability. The Diocese of North Carolina is unlike its sister dioceses to the East and the West in that it had all the big cities in the state: Charlotte, Raleigh, Greensboro, Winston-Salem, and Durham. As a result, its capacity to do things was so much larger than our diocese. Christ Church Charlotte had four thousand members, whereas there were only fifteen thousand Episcopalians in Western North Carolina. However, I never felt intimidated by Michael Curry, nor did I feel as if he were condescending or arrogant. At times, I felt envious. He was a natural leader who gathered people that trusted him and wanted to follow him. Five years ago, Michael asked Chip Marble, the retired bishop of Mississippi, to come to work for him. He and Chip shared the same kind of infectious laugh, and the two often joked back and forth. I envied that partnership and that looseness, because being a bishop is inherently lonely.

If I had those qualities, would I have stayed for the long haul? If I had Michael's team behind me, would I have lasted longer than twelve years as bishop? I doubted it. I had an impatience about bureaucracy, an aversion to time-wasting enterprises like much of these conventions, and a sickness over the necessary posturing that is required to use one's influence.

It took about forty-five minutes to count the ballots, and it took a while to gather everyone back in the sanctuary.

When all were present and the room was completely still, Katharine repeated her instructions about contacting the outside world: no calls, no tweets, no texts, no emails, nada. Nedi and I looked at each other. "Here we go," I whispered to her.

Katharine said, "For an election, a bishop needs 89 votes to be elected; 174 votes were cast." Her voice was formal, a little stiff. "Tom Bridenthal, 19 votes. Michael Curry, 121 votes."

Before she continued with the other two names, everyone knew Michael was elected. He had thirty-two more votes than he needed. Yet the place was still. We bishops have all been in a similar place before because we all live public lives. We knew we had made history in electing the first African American as the Presiding Bishop, and while we weren't afraid of it, we wanted to savor this moment, maybe because we knew how fast the future would come and maybe because there is just a sheer deep goodness in changing the world.

Katharine kept speaking. "Ian Douglas 13. Dabney Smith 21."

Then there was a roar of excitement, and everyone was on their feet, laughing, crying, and clapping. Tears streamed down my face. I held up my arms over my head and kind of twirled around to give thanks for the goodness of the Lord. "Whoa," I screamed. I turned to Nedi, and she was crying as well, and we embraced one another. I felt as if God were holding me and saying, "It is good; it is very good."

I thought Michael would win, but by a hundred votes? The place was a mass of shouting, crying, whooping, and clapping.

I looked at Tom Bridenthal, and he was smiling and clapping. So was Dabney Smith. I couldn't see Ian Douglas, but I could see Michael in the back of the church. He was trying to make his way to the front, but people were hugging him and reaching out to touch him.

When Michael got to the front, he and Katharine stood in the aisle and locked arms and slowly wheeled one another around almost like school children. They were simultaneously laughing and weeping.

Finally, Michael stood in the front, holding a hand mic.

"First," he said, his voice muffled by his emotions, "I want to tell you how much I respect my brother nominees. We love one another and when we were in New York, having dinner together, we said we'd all be proud to serve anyone at this table. So, thank you Tom and Dabney and Ian."

We clapped.

"Then," he said, "I give thanks for this church because it's the church that taught me about Jesus. It's a good church; it's a Spirit led church, and it's

God's church. I am honored and humbled to serve God and to serve you as your next Presiding Bishop."

"And finally," he said, "I want to thank Bishop Katharine for her leadership and her dignity and her strength. She has had to bear a lot in these nine years, and she has done so with grace. And," he paused, "and you need to know that she is really cool. In fact, I am going to need some of her cool going forward."

"I love you; I love the church; I love the Lord. God Bless you."

And we stood and clapped again.

Then the organist began playing the hymn "Lift Every Voice and Sing."

*Sing a song full of the faith that the dark past has taught us,*
*Sing a song full of the hope that the present has brought us;*
*Facing the rising sun of our new day begun,*
*Let us march on 'til victory is won...*[3]

Michael Curry was elected because he had the skills and experience and was the right person for this time in the church. This was the time for what had been previously known as a white "country club" type of church to let go of that burden and open its doors to say, "God is here and giving us life" to all those who had given up on it, because they thought it was calcified in the past. When I finally got through the crowd to Tom Bridenthal, I said in his ear, "You can't fight a movement."

So, it was hugely symbolic, but it was beyond symbolism. People didn't seek out Michael Curry for advice or leadership because he was African American, but because his love of the Lord came through all he did. While as liberal as Bishop Katharine, Michael would be able to talk to churchgoers in Texas and New Orleans and Anglo-Catholic Wisconsin. He had the Lyndon Johnson love of people. He leaned into them when he talked, laughed with them, and encouraged their joy in a way that I never could.

There was something else about this for me. I needed to have someone I could believe in the way I believed in Katharine Jefferts Schori, and I needed a spiritual jolt because our church was in short supply of wonder. We have had our full dose of reality. We were shrinking in church attendance and were in an age of secularism. Because the dilemma we faced was complex and widespread, our response had been at best ineffective.

We didn't want more data about cultural trends. I was fed up with reality. I wanted the Holy Spirit to show up. I wanted the lame to walk and the blind to see and the dead church to come alive. I needed to believe in The Episcopal Church because as much as I loved parts of my office, the toll

---

3. Williams, *Lift Every Voice and Sing II*, 1.

of the last eleven years weighed on me: disciplining priests or intervening between low-functioning clergy and angry parish leaders. I was weary of raising money, and I was exhausted from being a visitor in everyone else's "church home."

The euphoria about Michael Curry was not an Obama echo. It wasn't "Change you can believe in," but there was a little of that. Some of Michael Curry's charisma is his voice. However, I had known him and worked with him for more than ten years, so if it was just glitter, I would have seen it. No, it was more.

I thought about my grandmother who played the organ at Trinity Episcopal Church in Asheville. Her father was a slave owner in Pinewood, South Carolina. If it had not been for the Great Depression, her family would still be on the plantation, living on the land that had been plowed by slaves. When I was a young boy, my brother and sister and I went to her house on Saturday mornings. She'd make pancakes on a wood-fired stove in the kitchen with a green linoleum floor. But with all the cozy memories comes a harsh one: I learned the N-word from my grandmother, and she said things then that haunt me today.

As I looked at Michael Curry, I thought of the Seamus Heaney poem:

*History says, don't hope*
*On this side of the grave.*
*But then, once in a lifetime*
*The longed-for tidal wave*
*Of justice can rise up,*
*And hope and history rhyme.*[4]

Maybe this was my once in a lifetime. I thought maybe Michael Curry's grandmother and my grandmother might be sitting together at the heavenly table on a green linoleum floor, drinking coffee, and giving their common benediction.

In the Cathedral the noise abated as the bureaucracy took over the proceedings. First the bishops from African descent came forward and signed the Testimonial, which is just sheets of paper signed by the bishops voting as a record for the Archives. There were about twenty of them crowded around a table. Then Katharine announced that all bishops had to sign, so we lined up.

Bishop Katharine told us that a message would go over to the House of Deputies back at the Convention Center giving the president the name and then the president would have to come back over to the Cathedral. "So," she

---

4. Heaney, *Cure of Troy*, 77.

said. "Don't leave the building, don't text, don't email, don't tweet. But you can take pictures."

Immediately Michael Curry was swarmed by bishops getting selfies or photos of him. I eased out of the aisle and put my arm around him and took a selfie of the two of us.

It was now past noon. We went into the parish hall where there were sandwiches.

When the president and her chancellor arrived, we gathered back in the church. The president smiled and waved. She was a formidable presence because she had a big personality. She was funny, but politically shrewd. Her chancellor looked very formal and lawyerly—less because of her clothes and more her demeanor. She looked ready for a courtroom.

The president made some official remarks and then began to escort Michael out, but he was no longer simply Michael. One of the bishops who was a large man and an ex-police officer, grabbed Michael's right arm and got a half step in front of him as his bodyguard. Michael was in the bubble.

We had to wait for the House of Deputies to confirm the election. We got the word that Michael was soon to enter the Convention Center to be presented to the rest of Convention. Most of us wanted to be present, so we loaded onto the bus. When I walked into to the cavernous space of the Convention Hall for the House of Deputies, there was a gauntlet of reporters and people. There was a free-floating euphoria amid the mass of people with cameras and cell phones. I was soon immersed in a pack of people and couldn't move.

Suddenly there was a murmur, which built into a roar. Michael's handlers had used a side door and were coming up the aisle next to the far wall. The photographers started running. People were shouting and clapping. Some stood on their chairs straining to see. I guessed that at least three thousand people were in the room.

When at last Michael got to the microphone at the podium, he looked as if he had grasped what had happened. He took a deep breath as he waved both arms to the screaming crowd.

"Oh, God love ya," he said. "I know you haven't had lunch so, no sermons now. It really is a blessing and privilege to serve our church and to serve our Lord in this way," he said. "I treasure this church, this house, the House of Bishops, all of us. We are God's children."

He took a breath and looked around the vast room. The flashes from cameras were like the glints of the sun off the ripples on water. I wondered if he was going through his many past speeches for the words to say.

"This church is the church where I learned about Jesus. This is a good and wonderful church, and we are good and wonderful people, and I thank

God to be one of the baptized among you," Curry said. "My heart is really full."

"We've got a society where there are challenges before us and there are crises all around us. And the church has challenges before it," he said. "We got a God and there really is a Jesus, and we are part of the Jesus Movement. Nothing can stop the movement of God's love in this world."

As Michael left the platform, the crowd spontaneously began singing "Praise God, from Whom All Blessings Flow."

Afterward, I wandered back into the heat of Salt Lake City looking for somewhere to cool off and regroup. I was limp; too much was going on inside. I believed in Michael Curry, but I had believed in leaders before. I cared about him too much not to worry about what this office would do to his life and his family. Yes, I was glad to be getting out of the grind of the church machine, but I felt a pang of regret for not being able to be part of the change that Michael would bring. But the pang wasn't enough to change my course.

The true center of the church had grown so small for me—not the administration, not the appointments, not the canons, not the wrangling. The center was the bread, the wine, the Word, the people gathering to pray, the times when the world stops—burying the dead, anointing the sick, baptizing the converts. However, as bishop I seldom did those things, and I wondered how often Michael Curry would.

I realized it wasn't that I needed out of the church. I needed to find my way back in, but I couldn't get there with all the baggage of being the bishop. There was nothing wrong with the office, but it was just too narrow for me.

I found a Starbucks near the Convention Center and sat in the cool air drinking peppermint tea. I thought about Michael when I softly said this prayer: "May the enthusiasm you feel this day sustain you in the years to come. May those who grow to see you as the roadblock to their intended future, remember this day and be gracious."

Then I added, "And Dear God, lover of souls. I know you are with me even when I forget you, and I know this is your church even when I despair for its disappointments and my own. For all those who sometimes feel lost like me, give us hope, show us the way, and make us new."

# 14

## Getting Out

And somehow, as I struggle to change myself, the person I am with, the situation I am experiencing, I find that what I am looking for, what I am opening myself to, is that buried reality: God the Giver, who is never exhausted.

—Rowan Williams, *Being Christian: Baptism, Bible, Eucharist, Prayer*

"What's your driver? What's the thing that makes your pulse go faster? When do you find that you forget yourself because you love what you do?"

"You mean in my job?" I asked.

"No—not your job. Don't be too focused on church stuff Porter. What do you love? That's how you'll find your driver."

I stared at the speaker, but I wasn't focused on his slick brown hair.

I tried to remember what I had forgotten for most of the past eleven years because of being the bishop. I couldn't think of many drivers because mostly I felt as if I had been driven.

There I was at an Episcopal Retreat Center just outside Richmond, Virginia, attending a conference for Episcopal bishops who were considering retirement. It was October 2014.

I had made the decision to attend because no conversation can go on forever. Two months before in August, Jo and I were sitting on our back porch on a Sunday afternoon sharing the *New York Times*. I had just returned home from Hayesville, North Carolina, two hours away, and was so tired I was only reading headlines, flipping the newsprint from right to left faster and faster. I felt Jo bearing down on me.

"You can't see yourself, but I can. You can't even focus you're so exhausted." Her voice dropped an octave as she quietly addressed me by my nickname. "Bam, be honest. You weren't there for a lot of stuff with the kids, and now our grandson. The church has always come first. You know, it's not like we know how much time we have on this earth."

"I know," I said, and I did know. The sermon I gave that morning was the same one I gave somewhere else three years ago because I didn't have time to write a new one. I felt like Leslie Gore getting on the stage to sing "It's My Party" until she died. It wasn't that I hated my job, but that I felt constrained—stuck in the bishop bubble—as if the purple clerical shirt defined me like some superhero—except I had lost my alter identity. I was Batman without ever escaping to be Bruce Wayne.

"Okay," I said, putting down the paper and turning to look at Jo face to face. "Let's say 2016. I'll do one more Convention next November, but I'll quit before November 2016. How about that?"

"How about today?" Even as she said this, she started to smile and she got up, held my face with her two hands and softly kissed me. As she backed away, she whispered, "Thank you."

I found that it's just as hard to get out of being a bishop as it is to become one. When I talked to the bishop in charge of transitions, he told me I should attend a conference on "Orderly Transitions" which sounded like an oxymoron. This brought me to Richmond, Virginia, listening to the speaker ask me about my driver.

"Drivers are your motivators. Put all financial considerations aside and ask yourself, 'Why do I work? What's the pull for me?' We've given you a list of suggestions for your passions so check the ones that click for you."

We were sitting in a circle—the facilitator and his wife, thirteen bishops and nine spouses in a large antiseptic conference room. I knew everyone because there are only a few more than a hundred active bishops, and we see each other twice a year. None of my close friends were present, but I was comfortable with everyone there. I was seated next to a bishop from the Midwest. At my first bishop's meeting she sat beside me at dinner and said, "I like you already because I heard you're a Yellow Dog Democrat." She had an elegance about her—blonde hair, a beautiful singing voice, and a wonderful light laugh. She leaned over and said, "What if everything's your driver?"

"Then you need to retire because you are overworking," I said.

My top choices from the list of drivers were: "to belong, to develop friendships, to be constantly learning, to have exposure to people" (even though I wasn't sure what that meant), "to be connected, and to be valued." I did not check things like "to have accomplishments, to be an authority figure, to wield power, or to have visibility" but I thought maybe I was being Southern about this—sublimating my selfish motives to look better. There was no box for "to get out."

"This is a starting place," the leader said. "We'll come back to this later."

That afternoon we watched the film *The Bucket List*. I didn't get it. The leaders handed out a sheet with questions like "I want to visit____?" or "I have a wild desire to ____?" All I could think of was, "I have a wild desire to do something that is me." I didn't want to go to Europe or go hang gliding. I didn't want more diversions. I wanted inversions: to cut out so much of the ceremonial and administrative activities that were just not who I was.

The next day, the female speaker was in charge. Unlike the male speaker, she was vivacious, elflike—short, funny, and energetic. "Think about your drivers and then look at this list of what you do as bishops," she said, pointing to her PowerPoint. "Contrast your passions with what you actually do. Take the top five drivers or passions and then ask yourself what activity in your future retirement would fill that need."

I circled "Communications." I then linked it to the driver "Be Creative" and then wrote "Write a book." We worked for a half hour. My list was "Write a book; conduct retreats; teach; be a spiritual director; volunteer to teach kids to read."

She clapped her hands and said, "Now we've put newsprint on the walls. Go find a sheet and draw a picture of your future."

I drew a picture of a book cover and then added a dollar sign on the front because claiming the desire to be a writer seemed ethereal. Bishops are always writing books about how the church should work, but that wasn't my book. I wanted to read my life to understand how I had gotten here and where I was called to go. When I sat down, I realized everyone else was still drawing.

One bishop wanted to build a canoe; another wanted to travel to Florence; another wanted to spend time with her grandchildren. No one wanted to do anything with the church.

One of the spouses drew a picture of a man and woman sitting next to each other. When we explained our drawings, I said, "I want to write a bestseller," but felt sheepish when the spouse said, "I want to get to know my husband again."

The afternoon of the last day, I had an hour with the bishop in charge of the retirement process. It felt as if I had gone full circle. Ten years ago, this bishop and his wife came to our house in Athens, Georgia, two weeks after my election to tell me what it meant to be a bishop. Now I was sitting across a circular table in the large dining room asking him to tell me how to get out.

He leaned back and ran his hand through his thick brown hair. Smiling he said, "Porter, figure out when you want to be done and then count back eighteen months minimum."

"That doesn't work," I said. "I want to be done before eighteen months. In fact, I am so done right now."

"Well. You are part of a system and it's a slow system. You need to get on the Presiding Bishop's calendar and work backward. So, call the PB's administrative assistant and fix a date about two years from now for the new bishop to be ordained."

I turned my head and looked out the far window of the dining hall. "Shit," I whispered. I had been offered a job in Virginia the year before which I turned down to "do the right thing" by not deserting the diocese in the middle of the night, but I had no idea that this decision would stick me with staying for two more years.

I took a breath and looked at him. He had moved into his professional mode. His square jaw told me we were getting down to it.

"Okay. I'll call her. What's next?"

He glanced at his notes. "Well, you need to tell your staff and you need to tell the Standing Committee of the diocese since they are in charge of the election. When you find a date from the Presiding Bishop for the new bishop to be ordained, count back three months from the election of the new bishop. Then count back about a year for the nominating process and then count back about three months for your announcement."

"That's a lot of arithmetic," I said. "Let's talk hypothetical. Suppose I retire in October of 2016. What then?"

"Well. You'd have an election in June 2016; you'd announce early in 2015; and you'd tell your staff at the end of this year."

"Done." I left the dining hall, went to my room, and called the Presiding Bishop's assistant.

"Porter," she said, "the Presiding Bishop will be in Asheville on October 1, 2016. Details will follow."

I could see the exit, but it was two years away.

\* \* \*

The last night of the Orderly Transition Conference I couldn't sleep—too many possibilities; too many loose ends; too many hopes and regrets. Finally, at four thirty in the morning I got up, showered, dressed, and started driving home. I arrived at the office around ten o'clock.

I had seen on my phone that the Presiding Bishop's assistant had emailed me a confirmation that the ordination date for October 1, 2016 was solid. I wanted to print this off and delete it from my email because my assistant monitored this email. I didn't want her to know my plans before the rest of the staff. I intended to tell them at our staff retreat in December.

She was the only person in the office. After greeting her, I told her I needed to do something and then we could catch up.

I pulled up the email, pressed print, and then went into Lisa's office.

She was fifteen years younger than me and a natural born caretaker. Trained as a counselor, she could use her slow mellow cadence to quiet the most anxious caller. When I first met her, I was surprised when she stood up because at almost six feet, she looked me eye to eye.

We talked about my visitation to a parish on Sunday and went through the mail. She asked me to sign some checks.

After about half an hour, I said, "Okay, I'll see you Monday morning."

I was almost home when I slapped the steering wheel. "Shit. Shit. Shit." I had left the letter from the Presiding Bishop's assistant in the copier. So, I turned the car around and drove back.

When I opened the office door, my assistant was standing in the hall with a piece of paper in her hands.

"Anything you want to tell me?" she asked.

When we sat in my office across from one another, I said, "I'm sorry you found out this way. The truth is, I love working with you and the staff. You're my family. I'd do anything for you, but I can't do this anymore. It's just eating me up. I take pills to sleep. I have a personal trainer, a therapist, a spiritual director, and I am still not happy."

She wiped her tears with the back of her hand. Her face was flushed. We sat for a moment looking at each other.

She pushed her blonde hair away from her face and said, "We all knew you'd quit pretty soon, but we thought you'd stay at least until you're sixty-eight."

"I know. If I could, I would, but I just can't."

"So, how's this going to work?" she asked.

I started to go over the timetable with her.

"No," she said. "I mean what's going to happen to the staff?"

"Well, you're all wonderful people who work hard and accomplish a lot. I can't imagine you're in danger with your jobs, but the truth is the new bishop will do whatever she or he wants to."

We looked at each other. I said, "I hate that. I do."

"Well," she said, "you know I'm trying to be a deacon so I might just go out the same time as you."

We agreed that this would be our secret until the staff retreat in December. Though I was sorry for her burden, I was glad that someone in the office knew what was going on with me.

* * *

My senior year at Lee Edwards High School I was six feet two and weighed 185 pounds. In the fall, football was my life. I was the leading receiver and the cornerback on defense. I was on the kickoff team and the kickoff receiving team, which meant I was never off the field.

The third game of the season we almost lost a game to a team from Greensboro because in the last minutes they ran a kickoff back for a touchdown. At practice the next Monday afternoon the coach had us kneel on the ground. He was six feet two and relatively soft spoken. I liked him. He was a smart coach. He changed the offense, so we passed more, which meant I got the ball more often. We always had to run laps before and after practice, but it never seemed as if he were proving he was in charge. He was just trying to keep us in shape.

"Our kickoff team could have cost us the game gentlemen," he said, pushing his voice so we could hear him. "This is the simplest task we have—you run in your lane down the field. If everyone just does that, then there's no way the other team can score. It isn't rocket science; it's just a question of commitment."

Then he looked around the team—eye to eye with all the players on the kickoff team. "Is there anyone out here that doesn't want to be on this team?"

I don't know why I raised my hand, but I did. I was thinking, "Well, I never get off the field and I'd do better on offense and defense if I could rest just for a few minutes. Plus, someone else who doesn't start could play."

The coach's expression read "Are you kidding me?"

I screwed up. My teammates looked at me with heads cocked. I inhaled a deep breath and stood up. "Wait Coach. I got confused. I do want to be on the receiving team. I thought you were asking something else."

He still stared. "No, son. You raised your hand for a reason. You're off." He looked around the field and pointed. "Jimmy, you're now on kickoffs. You'll work with Coach McNair. Okay gentlemen, let's run to remember what we need to do to get focused for East Mecklenburg on Friday."

I tried to get to the coach as the other players put their helmets on and started around the track.

"Coach. I'm so stupid. I just didn't get it."

"Okay. Okay," he said, but his expression didn't say "okay." It said, "What the hell were you thinking?"

Then he said, "Run, Bam. Maybe that will get your head in the game."

The truth is I didn't miss being on the kickoff team, and I liked getting my breath back standing on the sideline. Plus, I don't think anyone scored on a return all year, so it didn't hurt the team. But I felt as if something was torn in my relationship with the coach and I wondered if my teammates thought I was either a prima donna for not being on the team or a dumbass for not reading the coach's nonverbal signals. It made me vow not to raise my hand again regardless of how tired the game made me.

* * *

The December staff retreat was hard. The women wept, and the men looked forlorn. "It's not about you," I said over and over. "I love being with you and working with you, but this job is killing me."

The office coordinator, asked, "Do we have to submit our resignations?"

As she said this, she shook her long black hair and bit her lower lip. She had been with me the longest and I knew how much the job meant to her.

"No," I said, but I couldn't give them any guarantees. The new bishop could do whatever he or she wanted.

The financial officer crooked her neck to her left shoulder and asked in her usual business voice, "What's it going to cost?"

"A lot," was all I could say.

We talked about what might happen to them with the new bishop. I tried to give them some assurance, but I couldn't. Even though the priest who was my assistant had known this for a week, I had a hard time looking at him. He had moved from Atlanta for this job and told me the first day, "I know I work for you, but the only way we can do this is if we are best friends." And we were. He had warned me how hard this day would be, but if anything, he had underestimated it.

Finally, someone said, "We get it. We work at the pleasure of the bishop."

* * *

In April 2016, the four nominees were announced. During the previous months I had no idea what was going on with the election process. The attention of the diocese was moving away from me. I was becoming increasingly irrelevant. I stopped generating new programs or initiatives. It would be like giving your child more advice before he or she goes to college. I still presided at all meetings. I still made my visitations on Sunday. However, even though I was determined to simply do what we had been doing for a decade, every Sunday was a series of "I'll never forget . . . " or "Remember when . . . " followed by "I can't believe you are leaving." It was exhausting, like going to your funeral Sunday after Sunday and hearing how much everyone missed the departed. I was touched by people's affection, but it was all past tense. The more they talked, the more I realized we weren't going to have a future together. Someone else would be their bishop. My photo might still be on the wall somewhere in their church, but underneath it would be *Bishop Porter Taylor, 2004–2016.*

I looked at the four names of the nominees. I knew one of them because she was a priest in the diocese. After I announced my resignation, she had talked to me about whether to run. I had a high respect for her. She was smart and dedicated and exceedingly honest. A former CPA, she knew how to make things work but had a pastoral side as well. When we talked, I told her, "You'd be great, but I don't know if you realize what a lonely office this is." She was the only one on the list I had even heard of before.

One priest was from a large church in Boston. I was impressed that the diocese nominated a candidate who was gay.

The third candidate was also from a large church and was from Houston. Finally, the last nominee was the assistant to the bishop of Oklahoma. He and the person from Houston both spoke Spanish which would be a huge plus in our diocese.

\* \* \*

Finally in mid-May the four candidates came to the diocese. Part of the election process is to have "walkabouts" or what we used to call "the dog and pony show." It's where the nominees visit parishes in different locations of the diocese to answer questions.

The evening before those were to begin, there was a Eucharist and dinner for the search committee, the nominees, the standing committee (the governing board of the diocese) as well as Jo and me. It happened to be the feast of Pentecost. We had a simple Eucharist at one of our chapels, and I preached. I had already preached that morning so I had a sermon prepared, but I realized I couldn't remain generic. These people had come for more than a Pentecost service.

What I found myself saying was this:

"If our vision narrows or our hearts grow cold or our minds close—and by 'our' I mean all of us—laity, deacons, priests, bishop—then it doesn't matter who gets elected. But if our vision is wide and our hearts warmed, and our minds opened—then it also doesn't matter who gets elected. What matters is our love of the Lord. What matters is that when we look at one another and the stranger, the face we see is Jesus Christ."

Of course, I was preaching to myself. I don't know if the nominees heard a word. I am sure they were wondering about the next few days when they would be grilled repeatedly throughout the diocese. I was telling myself, "You are not in charge of this. God is." That wasn't quite right. I was telling myself, "What happens next to the diocese is out of your hands." But what I knew in my heart was what happened next *was* out of my hands. Tonight, the task was to let go. One of these people would sit in my chair. When people started a sentence with "Bishop," they wouldn't be talking to me. I think I was telling myself that even though I would be part of the crowd now—with all the different tribes of non-bishops, maybe my heart would be opened. Maybe someone would look at me and see more than a man with no more titles or uniforms. Maybe I would sense the peace the world can't give, and the world can't take away.

When I looked at the four of them, I thought, "Where will I be once you are in my chair?"

* * *

Jo and I went to the session for the diocese to meet the candidates in Asheville. We sat in back. I only felt defensive on a few occasions. One nominee guaranteed they would make the half-time youth position full time. Another mentioned that they would strengthen the relationship of the diocese to the Cathedral. Everyone was asked about same-sex marriage, and two were asked about Cursillo which is part of the Renewal movement.

They all did well. Some better than others. It wasn't a matter of competency but more extrovert versus introvert and connecting with various special interests. Some thought before answering, and some just blurted out.

I had two thoughts. I kept remembering my experience twelve years ago—how exhausting it was to have strangers ask questions that often sounded as if they were asking about astrophysics. So much of it was like one of those bad dreams you have about realizing you have an exam but have not read the book. Second, I remembered the sincerity of people and realized that was true here as well. They genuinely cared for the church and took their responsibility to vote for a new bishop extremely seriously.

The next day I had a private meeting with the four of them. I told them about our finances and how I had worked for years to erase a five-million-dollar debt on the Conference Center. I gave them a spreadsheet of the diocese's finances. I talked about the clergy transitions coming up and told them about the staff.

They asked me several questions:

"What's the financial state of the diocese?"

"How vibrant is the youth program?"

"Is the Conference Center financially viable?"

"What day do you take off?"

Overall, the nominees seemed assured and confident. No one seemed nervous, but some seemed as if they were entering a territory without a map. I wondered if they really knew what a shift it would be if they were elected, and I felt an enormous amount of empathy.

Most of all, I wanted to say, "You have no idea what you are getting into and what the cost is." I wanted to say, "You know about the benefits and the stature one of you will gain. You know about all the glitter, but you have not a clue about what it's really like. You are going to be in a bubble that elevates but also isolates." I wanted to say, "Why don't you ask me why I am resigning?" But that wasn't what they wanted to know and probably didn't need to hear from me. They would learn it soon enough.

There was also an equal and opposite reaction. I had this strong sense of regret. "Why am I leaving all this?" I wondered. I meant my bishop friends, the conferences with engaging speakers, and interesting challenges. I meant the responsibility of steering the church in one direction and not another. I had voted for Katharine Jefferts Schori and Michael Curry. I had voted to depose two ultra conservative bishops. I had lunch with Rowan Williams. I had gone to the Lambeth Conference. Jo and I met the Queen of England, and then there were the people in Western North Carolina that I knew I wouldn't see anymore. And I meant the people I worked with who in truth were my only real friends. I meant the priests I admired and could have been friends with if not for my being their bishop.

I looked at these four eager priests and wondered if they would find a better way. When their time was done, what would they be saying to their successors?

* * *

The day of the election came. I walked into Trinity Church in downtown Asheville early in the morning of June 25, and for a moment was in a time warp. This was the church of my childhood. I stood by the pew my family sat in every Sunday in the 1950s and 1960s. I remembered at ten being an acolyte and the day the bishop came. I didn't secure the cross and during Bishop Henry's sermon it fell flat on the floor with a loud bang. I remembered when I was six and one Saturday morning when my mother was fixing the flowers for Sunday, I crept up and touched the long marble altar, afraid that I might get electrocuted from its power. I remembered my sister's wedding here and my mother's funeral here, and I thought "It's good to be here. It's good that it all ends here. It's good to come full cycle."

People filed in. There was a strange quietness to the murmurs and conversations. The clergy sat in pews on one side of the church and the lay delegates on the other. I sat at a table in the front between the choir stalls. Inside my jacket were the telephone numbers of the four nominees so I could call the eventual "Bishop Elect."

When the nominee from the diocese—the only nominee present—walked in, the day got deeper. She sat on the third row. I could see she was alone. I remembered the day wasn't just about an election; it was about people's lives. Since we hadn't started, I walked to a pew and said to a priest and friend of the nominee from the diocese, "Can you go sit with her? It's not a day to sit by herself."

Win or lose, I remembered how glad I was that my only audience on the day I was elected was my family.

We said the first part of the Eucharist and then after some housekeeping got to voting. To be elected, you had to have a majority of the laypeople's votes and a majority of the clergy's votes.

The first ballot made it clear that this was a two-person race: José McLoughlin and a priest from our diocese. One withdrew on this ballot, and another withdrew on the second. For the third ballot the magic numbers for election were sixty-nine clergy and sixty-four lay votes. The WNC candidate got seventy-three clergy but thirty-seven lay while José received fifty-four clergy and eighty-one lay. I knew what was going to happen. As counterintuitive as it seems, the clergy always follow the lay vote. For one reason, there are more of them and for another I assume if you talk to someone between ballots, you are talking more to the people in your parish than other clergy.

Before the fourth ballot I looked at the nominee from the diocese. This election was going to be whatever it would be. I thought she knew what was going to happen, and I wished I could excuse her for being in the church building when it did happen. I was tired of carrying out my salvation in public, and I grieved that this person was going through this in front of almost three hundred people.

While the tellers counted the ballots, we sang hymns. I later learned that I didn't turn off my microphone so everyone streaming the service at home got to hear me solo. I was sure that made their day.

There was this short span of time that stood still. The gap between inhalation and exhalation. The space when the world turns one way or another. As tired as I was, part of me hoped we would stay in this space—not because I wanted to be the bishop anymore, but I didn't want the pain to come to the diocesan candidate.

I read out the fourth ballot results. "Needed to win: sixty-nine clergy votes. Sixty-five lay votes."

The Very Rev. José McLoughlin sixty-nine clergy votes; eighty-six lay. There was a moment when no one moved or spoke and then the church erupted in cheers and clapping. In a moment the organ started, and we sang the Doxology: "Praise God from Whom All Blessings Flow."

The technicians came in and we called him on the phone connected to the speaker system so all could hear. He said all the right things. He was humbled by the trust placed in him and excited by the possibilities of what the diocese would do together. He had gifts I didn't have—an extravert with managerial skills, fluency in Spanish—and he had been working for the bishop of Oklahoma, so he already knew the drill.

But I wasn't thinking about the new bishop. I was thinking about the candidate sitting in front of me. The other two candidates who were not elected were in their homes, licking their wounds in private. But here she was with a church full of people who were clapping for someone else.

When everything quieted down, I felt something move inside and I walked to the front of the chancel and looked at her and said, "I just want to say thank you. You have conducted yourself with grace and with faithfulness and with deep integrity. And whatever the numbers say, you need to know how much we respect you, how much we admire you, and how much we love you."

I didn't know where the emotional wave came from. Part of it was that I knew her and had worked with her. But there was something deeper— something about how the church is structured. Its way of being church always deals with separation. We say, "One Lord, One Faith, One Baptism. One God and Father of all," but we are seldom one. Looking at the nominee, I could see her pain of not being elected. I wanted to say to her, "But you do not know the pain of being elected." The way this church is organized puts us in boxes and we color code the bishop's box with purple shirts. Yes, I believed in the boxes and yes, I was privileged to be in the bishop box, which allowed me to do so many important things. Yes. But from where I stood, I saw the pain of not being allowed into this box as well as the pain of getting in. Part of me was envious of the nominee who could go back to her parish, but I also knew I too would have been in pain if I had not been elected. We don't talk about sacrifice as Episcopalians, but we should. Every move is death and birth. Shedding one skin to take on another. Maybe I should have been a Quaker where we are all just friends, but no. Although I had felt and seen the wounds of hierarchy, I believed in the structure, but I could no longer grow in the bishop container, and because of that I couldn't do much good in this box anymore. I hoped in the days or weeks to come that the three not elected would celebrate the gift of being where they were, and I hoped José would find the episcopacy a good fit.

I went home, and Jo and I packed our car. We were to go to the beach for a month and let the ocean wash away all regrets and loose ends and wounds. Maybe a new future would become clear.

* * *

My last day as bishop was October 1, 2016 with the ordination of the new bishop. On an unseasonably warm November afternoon, my cell phone rang, and a voice said, "Porter, I've figured out your retirement."

"Sorry?" I asked.

He identified himself and then said, "Last Sunday I was talking to Gail O'Day, the dean of the seminary at Wake Forest. I mentioned you were retiring, and she said, "He should come and work for us.""

"Well," I said. I couldn't figure out why he was calling me. I didn't know him well. We were always courteous to one another.

Neither of us said anything for a few moments; then I remembered my manners. "This is so kind of you to think of me. I'll contact her."

"Do. You'd be a natural and you'll love Gail. She's probably the lone Episcopalian in the sea of the Baptists but since she's the dean, that's all that counts."

A few months later, Jo and I found ourselves in what looked like a subdevelopment of red brick buildings but was in fact the campus of Wake Forest Divinity School in Winston-Salem, North Carolina. I was to have a tryout at the seminary by preaching at their community worship and talking to students about discernment.

I had spoken several times with Chris, my faculty "handler" on campus.

"Should I bring vestments?" I asked.

"Since we are Baptists, if you want any, you should bring them," he said.

To get to the Divinity School, Jo and I walked through Wait Chapel, a cavernous space that seated over two thousand. It was stark. White walls, clear windows, auditorium seats, two aisles down the middle. It felt like my high school auditorium on steroids.

In contrast, the Divinity School Chapel was intimate, probably seating a hundred. I put on my white robe and a white stole. I had other vestments in my case—including my miter (bishop's hat)—but decided this was probably more than enough to convey I wasn't Baptist. My gold cross sparkled on my chest.

There was an altar with a loaf of bread and two chalices of red wine. A crowd streamed in at the last minute. The seminarians were so young; maybe a third under thirty and almost half African American. There was no procession. I just walked in with everyone else and took a seat on the first row. Jo was two rows back.

When the music started, I knew we had left our proper Episcopal hymnal. A short white woman played the piano like Jerry Lee Lewis. She didn't bob her head; her whole torso jerked up and down to the pounding of her hands.

"He is alive. He is not dead," we sang. I looked over my shoulder. Students clapped while they sang. Some raised their hands and waved their arms back and forth.

My sermon wasn't my best. I tried too hard to be erudite. Whenever I made a point that connected with the congregation, someone would shout "Yes Sir," or "Preach it," or my favorite, "Go Bishop."

It was so not where I lived, but it felt so right. I wasn't sure about doing this every week, but on this day it felt electric. It felt authentic—maybe because no one was saying the same lines they said last week and last year; maybe because there was more of a connection with the ministers and the congregation. I remember my daughter complaining about going to church when she was ten. "You get to sit up front and do all the fun stuff while everyone else has to sit and watch."

Here there was little "up front" versus "out there" and there wasn't much sitting and watching.

That afternoon Jo and I sat side by side in the Dean's office. The Dean was in her early sixties with an infectious laugh. I had heard she was smart—a New Testament Scholar who had come to Wake Forest from Emory. However, she didn't look detached from the everyday world like some academics.

"Porter and Jo. We'd love you to come here. Porter, of course, we'd need you to teach the Episcopal classes—things like The Book of Common Prayer and Episcopal Governance, but we'd love you to teach courses you are passionate about like Literature and Theology and Spirituality."

Jo and I looked at each other.

"What about Jo?" I asked. "Any art classes here?"

"Yes, but honestly UNC-Greensboro is so fabulous, you'd probably do better there. But certainly, you could take the undergraduate classes here if you want."

As we talked, I felt lighter. Yes, I was a little intimidated. I hadn't been in the classroom full time in over twenty years, and though I knew a lot about being an Episcopalian and had been to seminary, I didn't feel qualified to teach all that the Dean was asking. But I felt at home in this environment and something about the Dean made me trust her.

That trust went deeper when she said, "You need to know that I have a form of cancer. It's in my brain, but the doctors are optimistic." I was moved. In the face of her mortality, she was leading a seminary and trying to start a new program in Episcopal Studies, and she was inviting me along. As I gazed at her, my mundane concerns evaporated. She was dealing with more than course selections. I didn't know if this was where we'd come, but if we did, it would be good.

As we were leaving, I reached over to shake her hand. "I hope this works," she said. "It'd be fun for everyone."

As Jo and I walked back toward our Subaru, she said, "What do you think?"

"I don't know what to think," I said, "but at least we know there's a doorway to get out of bishop world, and that's a good thing."

* * *

Wake Forest was a blessing, a new beginning. In my first class I was challenged because I said "Brothers and sisters" as a greeting. The Academic Dean told me, "We have students who are in transition. Find a way not to limit people to gender boxes."

"Oh," I said, and wondered what world I was now in. But in the weeks and months that followed, I discovered a richness outside Episcopal world. I discovered my narrative preaching has little to do with much of the preaching in African American churches. I discovered all my favorite poets are white and their wisdom is miles away from my students' hunger. I discovered that theology unconnected to the world is stuck in a book and doesn't animate or transform students' lives.

I discovered that my world had been vanilla since high school.

And so, while I had the title of "Visiting Assistant Professor for Episcopal Studies," I was the one going to school. And I marveled at the lessons I learned. Lessons from one student who after classes worked in a UPS warehouse until three in the morning. Lessons from a student who the year before Wake Divinity was in a shelter. Lessons from another student who told me that she found Jesus when she stopped snorting cocaine.

I had prayed to get out of the bishop bubble into the real world, and here it was. Yet I also rediscovered my love of church—of Sunday corporate prayer, of opening my hands to receive the bread of heaven instead of feeding myself at the altar, of drinking from the cup of salvation, of being fed by someone else's sermons that are deep and wise. Yes, I still yearned to preach and did on occasion. I missed my bishop friends and found ways to connect when I could.

But what I found is that God is not someone I need to talk about as if I am an expert and that the church is not something I need to run as if it's a business. Because I was set free, for me God has been set free. Because the church is not something I police; on its best days it's just a vehicle for grace. On Sundays I come in, sit down, and pray that my heart might be opened. I listen for Good News in the sermon and always give thanks when I eat the bread and drink the wine.

When I left seminary in 1993 and moved back to Nashville, the head mover said to me as he was loading the truck with all our stuff, "Well it looks like you're going back to where you started, ain't you?"

I could have said the same thing to myself, but it's not quite true. Yes, I am still a sinner in need of redemption. I am still a lost soul in need of being found. But here's the thing. I give thanks for all that God has done for me and to me. On my honest days, I have no regrets.

What I have learned is this. Our lives are short. My time as the bishop was the blink of an eye. My regret is in not saying more about things that matter—like social justice; like the wideness of God's mercy; like our common need for confession, forgiveness, and repentance; like our calling to be present in the world's joys and sorrows. I regret wasting so much time being the mayor or police officer or judge of the diocese and not being a simple God lover.

But my regrets are much smaller than my thanksgivings for the privilege of being part of major transitions in people's lives. My greatest appreciation is that through the rough and tumble of the episcopacy, some of my defenses got shaved down. Through my many internal and some external struggles, I remembered what mattered and what didn't. If your need is to be liked, being the bishop was a perfect antidote because the purple shirt is a magnet for projections. My thanks is not for the pain that caused, but for the transformation that evoked. At the end, all we have is the love of God. And at the beginning all we have is the love of God, and what we have to learn, and what I learned but often forget is that all the time—when we are in our "I am important" suit or simply in the clothes that say "Here I am, the clod of dirt God created," all we have is the love of God.

What I have learned—albeit not quickly or easily—is that's enough.

# Bibliography

Berthier, Jacques. "Veni Sanctus Spiritus." In *Music from Taize*, 68–70. Chicago: GIA Publications, 1981.

Bourgeault, Cynthia. *Centering Prayer and Inner Awakening*. Lanham, MD: Cowley, 2004.

Colledge, Edmund, and James Walsh, eds. *Julian of Norwich Showings*. The Classics of Western Spirituality. New York: Paulist Press, 1978.

Griffiths, Bede. *Universal Wisdom: A Journey through the Sacred Wisdom of the World*. San Francisco: HarperSanFrancisco, 1994.

Heaney, Seamus. *The Cure of Troy: A Version of Sophocles Philoctetes*. New York: Farrar, Straus & Giroux, 1961.

Intrator, Sam M., and Megan Scribner, eds. "The Truly Great," In *Leading from Within: Poetry that Sustains the Courage to Lead*, 123. San Francisco: Jossey-Bass, 2007.

James, William. *The Principles of Psychology*, Volume 2. New York: Dover, 1950.

Julian of Norwich. *All Will Be Well*. Edited by John Kirvan. 30 Days with a Great Spiritual Teacher. Notre Dame, IN: Ave Maria, 2008.

Keating, Father Thomas. "The Welcoming Prayer." https://crossministrygroup.org/wp-content/uploads/2019/06/R-Group-Process-Welcoming-Prayer.pdf.

Lawrence, D. H. "Edgar Allan Poe." In *Studies in Classic American Literature*, 29. London: Penguin Classics, 1990.

Merton, Thomas. *New Seeds of Contemplation*. Boston: Shambala, 1961.

———. *The Seven Storey Mountain*. New York: Harcourt, Brace, 1948.

Millay, Edna St. Vincent. "Dirge Without Music." In *The Norton Anthology of Modern Poetry*, edited by Richard Ellman and Robert O'Clair, 493. New York: Norton, 1973.

Nye, Naomi Shihab. "The Art of Disappearing." In *Words Under the Words: Selected Poems*, 29. Portland, OR: Eight Mountain, 1995.

Rolheiser, Ronald. *Sacred Fire: A Vision for a Deeper Human and Christian Maturity*. New York: Image, 2014.

Rumi. "Out Beyond Ideas of Wrongdoing and Rightdoing." In *The Essential Rumi*, translated by Coleman Barks, 36. Edison, NJ: Castle, 1997.

Saint John of the Cross. *Dark Night of the Soul*. Translated by Mirabai Starr. New York: Penguin Group, 2002.

St. Augustine. "On the Anniversary of His Ordination." In *The Works of Saint Augustine: A Translation for the 21st Century*, edited by John E. Rotelle, 292–94. Brooklyn, NY: New City, 1990–97.

St. Bonaventure. *The Life of Saint Francis.* Translated by E. Gurney Salter. 1904. London: J.M. Dent, 1932.

Sewell, Elizabeth. *Signs and Cities.* Chapel Hill, NC: The University of North Carolina Press, 1968.

Sexton, Anne. "The Saints Come Marching In." In *The Complete Poems,* 470. Boston: Houghton Mifflin, 1981.

Shannon, William H., ed. *The Hidden Ground of Love: The Letters of Thomas Merton on Religious Experience and Social Concerns.* New York: Farrar, Straus & Giroux, 1985.

Soren Kierkegaard, Journalen JJ:167(1843), *Soren Kierkegaards Skrifter,* Soren Kierkegaard Research Center, Copenhagen, 1997--, volume 18, page 306.

*The Book of Common Prayer.* New York: Church Publishing, 1979.

Thurman, Howard. *The Inward Journey.* Richmond, IN: Friends United Press, 2007.

Underhill, Evelyn. *Practical Mysticism.* San Bernardino, CA: Renaissance Classics, 2012.

Williams, Arthur B., et al., eds. "Lift Every Voice and Sing," In *Lift Every Voice and Sing II: An African American Hymnal,* 1. New York: The Church Hymnal Corporation, 1993.

Williams, Rowan. *Being Christian: Baptism, Bible, Eucharist, Prayer.* Grand Rapids, MI: Eerdmans, 2014.

Yeats, W. B. "Easter 1916." In *The Collected Poems of W.B. Yeats,* 180. New York: Macmillan, 1956.